BON VOYAGE:

AN ASTROLOGICAL STUDY OF RELOCATION

MARC PENFIELD

American Federation of Astrologers, Inc.
PO Box 22040 6535 South Rural Road
Tempe, AZ 85285-2040

First Printing: 1992
ISBN Number: 0-86690-407-0
Library of Congress Catalog Number: 91-77008

Cover layout: Lynda Kay Fullerton

Published by:
American Federation of Astrologers, Inc.,
P.P. Box 22040, 6535 South Rural Road,
Tempe, Arizona 85285-2040

THIS BOOK IS DEDICATED TO

VICTORIA SHAW

a beautiful actress and assiduous
researcher with Moon in Aquarius and
Jupiter in the ninth house

and

VIOLA HUERTA

my travel agent and fellow globetrotter
with Sun in Aquarius and Jupiter in
Sagittarius

whose penetrating insight and
understanding caused me to realize that
relocation affects our destiny in more
ways than I could have ever imagined

and special thanks to

JUDY JOHNS

fellow astrologer from Aquarius
Workshops in Los Angeles for the use of
her computer

TABLE OF CONTENTS

LIST OF FIGURES

LIST OF TABLES

INTRODUCTION

WHAT IS RELOCATION?

Relocation is the study of an individual's reaction to a specific environment and the circumstances they will encounter during the time spent in a specific locale. Some events or occurrences may also be predicted in advance, along with highlighting areas which will require added attention. Relocation may be used in many ways: by persons wishing to excel in a particular field or to experience events denied to them in their current place of residence. Corporations wishing to relocate employees into more productive areas are prime candidates for relocation analysis as are students wishing to further their education. Tourists seeking the ideal vacation spot would do well to investigate relocation as would retirees contemplating the ideal spot in their declining years. The planets and aspects in the relocated chart are identical to those in the natal chart: only the house positions of the planets have changed as have those planets aspects to the angles of the horoscope, the Ascendant and Midheaven.

I first heard of relocation through Jim Lewis, the founder of ASTRO*CARTO*GRAPHY, some years ago. Having worked in the travel industry for many years plus residing in many corners of the USA made me an excellent guinea pig for research. The eminent Canadian astrologer, L.E. Johndro, figured that location played a major role, anywhere from 25%-75%, in determining the amount of success one could expect from life. Obviously, some people are more susceptible to electro-magnetic forces than others, so it makes it very important for them to choose a compatible area.

Johndro felt that humans were like radio sets: some people have higher frequencies than others. If you're getting too much static on your set, simply move it to a more favorable site where the reception is better. Not only will you pick up new stations, but your audience will be different. After researching how relocation has affected hundreds of famous people and close personal friends, I'm totally convinced that location is a major factor in one's choice of vocation, not to mention the completion of your destiny or karma. Moving from one locale to another simply adjusts the lens of your camera: some areas which were formerly out on the periphery are now dead-center while other areas that were once of extreme importance now assume a secondary role.

A friend of mine put it another way, by using the analogy of a houseplant. Many organisms are unfortunately placed on the wrong side of a house: some ferns are mistakenly located on the south side where they often wither and die from extreme heat or too much exposure to the sun. Other plants on the shady side of the house never reveal their potential as they've been placed into an environment for which they were not intended. Plants respond to human contact and concern as well: some people do indeed have a "green thumb" and can make any endeavor prosper and thrive. Other people can't make a weed grow. Many individuals feel as if they're that plant on the wrong side of the house or that beautiful flower which receives little care or attention. By simply moving the organism, or person, into a more favorable environment you have thus changed their "life cycle" and reaction to their surroundings. But whenever relocation occurs, there's an initial shock or trauma as the organism adjusts to its new place in the world. Before too long, if the move was a wise one, that organism will begin to live life to its fullest extent instead of just taking up space on this planet. For some people, it's like having radical cosmetic surgery: inside we're still the same person but the reactions we receive from others changes our self-image. Astrologically, once a Virgo, always a Virgo. One always hopes that your best locale is on land and not out in the middle of an ocean. This would be fine if you're a shark or a piece of plankton but hopeless unless you're living on a yacht or life raft.

One could also use the analogy of a house to illustrate how relocation affects one's outlook on life. Most houses have many rooms, some of them more lived-in than others. It's the same in your horoscope: some houses are more occupied than others. If there's a particular room in your house that you would like to become more acquainted with, or even a room you would like to redecorate, then all you have to do is to go someplace where that room becomes an integral part of your existence. Geminians may want a larger library, Cancerians may want a more modern kitchen while Scorpios could desire a master bedroom instead of a sofa or small cot. By relocating, you will have redesigned the exterior environment but your inner shell remains the same. A brick house in New York remains a brick house even when moved to Los Angeles. You can add a second floor or an additional room onto the mainframe by ripping up walls and adding square feet, but the foundation basically remains identical. Just imagine what the London Bridge would say if it could talk when it was moved from foggy old London into the searing heat of the Arizona desert?

Some individuals, unfortunately, have little to say regarding where they will live. For children, the choice is often made by their parents, or sometimes by the courts. Many in the work force are transferred with little foresight as to how that new environment affects their potential to produce profits for the company. Most actors will have to go where the action is, either New York or Los Angeles in order to hit the "big time." Those involved in politics will have to live in the county seat, state capital or in Washington, DC. An expert welder or steel maker would be wise to live in a city which contains a steel mill or foundry and forget Hollywood or Honolulu where that type of work is scarce. Most people when relocating may have to choose another line of work lest they be left out in right field collecting welfare or unemployment. Those in the military are at the mercy of the government and have little say in where they will reside. About the only people who really have carte blanche to pick and choose are those contemplating retirement or a vacation spot, or those fortunate enough to be self-employed in a field which is in high demand.

As previously stated, relocation won't change your planets or the aspects between them: only the house positions of the planets and their aspects to the angles change. For instance, if you were born in Chicago and wanted to see what life in San Francisco would be like, simply subtract two hours from your birthtime as San Francisco, which is in the Pacific Time Zone, is two hours behind Chicago which is on Central Standard Time.

If you decide to move east to New York or Boston, then you would have to add one hour onto your birthtime as the East Coast is on Eastern Standard Time which is one hour in advance of Chicago. Your Midheaven and Ascendant will change, even if you move only a few miles from your birthplace and the aspects made to the angles of the horoscope will change as well.

The first thing to do after your relocation chart has been calculated is to ascertain the number of aspects being made to the angles of the relocated chart. One very important fact: use only a THREE-DEGREE ORB, nothing more, nothing less. Over the years I've found the 3-degree orb works all the time and larger orbs implant an ambiguity I would prefer to avoid. Here in the USA, one degree of longitude equals about 60 miles, becoming slightly less as one moves north to the Canadian border.

The second thing to note is which house now holds the ruler of your natal Ascendant. Its location will determine the nature of your existence in that locale, while the sign (which hasn't changed) will show how you accomplish that goal. When I moved from my birthplace in Chicago to Los Angeles, the ruler of my natal Ascendant (Gemini) moved from the fifth house to the sixth. Life in Chicago was one big party and my creativity ran rampant. Here in Los Angeles, Mercury in Scorpio sits in my relocated sixth house making me more research-oriented and health conscious.

I generally use Porphyry house cusps in relocation work. The MC and ASC are identical to those given in Placidus or Koch tables, but the distance between the MC and ASC is divided by three making the house cusps considerably different that other house systems which seem to be distorted, especially at high latitudes. In my opinion, however, Placidus does seem to do quite well when doing a psychological analysis of an individual while Koch works fantastically well when trying to predict events. If pos-

2

sible, try and keep the ruler of your natal ASC out of the sixth, eighth or twelfth houses, as those areas often present more problems than most individuals are prepared to deal with, like incarceration, death or massive transformation or health problems which continually need to be corrected.

The most important aspect any planet can make to an angle is the conjunction. The power of a planet is intensified whenever it's rising or setting or sitting at the top or bottom of the chart. Your life in that place where a planet conjuncts an angle is likely to take on the nature of that planet to a great degree. From my research, however, I've found that only 75% of the famous people in my files who made their name in a specific locale actually had a planet on an angle. The remaining 25% had other aspects like the sextile, square, trine or inconjunct. Conjunctions meld and merge the energy of any two bodies into a single unit, and don't forget that oppositions are also conjunctions as well. Thus in Section II, I don't list oppositions to the ASC or MC, only conjunctions to the DESC or IC. Sextiles indicate opportunities that may be found in your new locale while trines illustrate facility of expression and general ease. Squares show where frustration is likely to occur and stress or tension will surface wherever inconjuncts, or quincunxes, tend to predominate.

I love the inconjunct aspect and I use it extensively in my work. I've found this fascinating, but little used, aspect to indicate why some things continually go awry. There's always something in the inconjunct which necessitates repair, adjustment, alteration or elimination. I think of the inconjunct as the "glitch" in one's chart, the reason why the engine continually keeps getting clogged up. It's the "fly in the ointment" aspect which relates to the sixth and eighth houses. Whenever this aspect is powerful in your chart, there's always a danger of sickness or surgery: something has to be realigned or cut out in order for that organism to function at peak efficiency. A great deal of intensity is also present which might explain why those who have this aspect prominent in their chart often go overboard in certain areas of their life.

I don't use the semisquare or sesquare (sesquiquadrate) in my work as I don't have enough reliable data from which to draw a definitive conclusion. If you feel you're qualified enough to interpret these aspects, however, please feel free to do so. It appears that a semisquare is a weak square, acting like an itch that simply won't go away. It shows simple frustrations, minor irritations and petty annoyances we all encounter. If you scratch long and hard enough, the itch might disappear or you could end up with a severe abrasion or rash. The sesquare is what I call the "third base" aspect, a combination of the square and the semisquare. It has neither the agitation of the square nor the frustration of the semisquare but appears to operate on the mental level, rather than on the physical or emotional plane. I don't generally use them in my work as they place too much emphasis on what some call "hard aspects" which are largely stress producing. There are many times when we simply want to kick back, relax and view the scenery. After all, at Club Med who needs frustration or irritation?

I feel that aspects made to the Sun, Moon, Mercury, Venus and Jupiter are basically positive. You may disagree with me, but then a lot depends on the aspects between those planets in the natal chart. Aspects made between Mars, Saturn, Uranus, Neptune and Pluto are largely stress-producing and filled with tension. Sometimes you may need a jolt from these planets in order to get you out of that rut which prompted you to move in the first place. But I would tend to steer clear of any place where these aspects kept kicking me in the butt and kept my life on edge. I like to place to "good" planets on angles while keeping those "bad" planets as far from the angles as possible. But then there are individuals who seem to revel in misery and misfortune and are gluttons for punishment. As the French say, it takes all kinds and to each his own.

People have asked me how long it takes to feel the effects of relocating. It really depends on the natal chart. Fixed-sign types generally take longer to feel any change in their lifestyle while mutable sign types might feel a change in a week or less. Cardinal signs

3

seem to fall in the middle, but there's no hard and fast rule. If you can recall how long it took for you to become accustomed to that new person in your life or how long it took you to acquaint yourself with your new job, you already have a clue as to the length of time in question.

One final thing should be mentioned before you move. There are some people who should never move from the place of their birth, especially if they have Venus or Jupiter sitting in their fourth house. One should never move a benefic from an angle into a succedent or cadent house where its ability to grant favors is severely limited. Obviously, if you have Saturn or Pluto in your natal fourth house, it would be wise to move as far from your birthplace as possible, and the sooner the better. Generally speaking, the most favorable direction to move is indicated by the positions of Venus and Jupiter in your natal chart. If your Jupiter is in the second house, move northeast, if Venus sits in your fifth, move northwest. If there's a benefic planet in your ninth house at birth, then residence in a foreign country might be advised. The reverse applies if you have a malefic there.

Section IV deals with geodetic types of charts. When you desire more information on a place than you feel the relocated chart can deliver, these types of charts are highly recommended. These types of charts must also be used for those unfortunate individuals who have no idea of their birthtime. Geodetic charts do have their limitations as they don't describe the individual at all, only the environment into which that person is placed and the affect those surroundings will have on them. Geodetic charts always have a "base" from which to erect the chart. The regular geodetic chart familiar to most astrologers was first popularized by Sepharial some decades ago. It marks regions of the earth in 30-degree segments from the Greenwich meridian which is called 0 degrees of Aries. The Pyramid System does the same, except its "baseline" is the Great Pyramid of Egypt which sits at 31E09, over a sign away from the former meridian.

The Johndro system uses a combination of your Sun's degree (natal or progressed) generally given in right ascension plus the increment of precession, plus or minus the longitude of the locality you're investigating. Geodetic charts continually fascinate me when trying to predict geological or meteorological events like hurricanes, tornadoes, volcanic eruptions or earthquakes. Unlike the relocated chart which shows a great deal of free will, the geodetic charts are somewhat fated or fatalistic, impersonal in their meaning and often leaving the individual feeling as if they're at the mercy of the environment or the elements of nature.

Section V deals with the Declination Chart which I invented some years back. It's derived from the declinations in your natal chart which are either north or south of the ecliptic. However, I take the liberty of multiplying those declination degrees and then putting them onto a world map. Like the geodetic system, it shows areas where success or failure may be found, but the declination charts are also fated by nature. Declination charts seem to indicate the types of people one encounters in a specific locale but doesn't seem to indicate events per se.

Sections VI and VII are what I call "fine tuning" the relocated chart. For example, let's say you have your Jupiter conjunct the IC along the 121st meridian west of Greenwich. Looking at the US map, one sees this line passes close to Seattle, Portland, San Francisco, Sacramento, Reno and Los Angeles. Supposing that climate is not your prime concern and that you're self-employed and can pick at will wherever you wish to live. Which town along that 121st meridian will most suit your domestic, professional, monetary or romantic needs? In order to ascertain which community along that line harmonizes best with your natal chart, you must look at the horoscopes of those cities which are close to your Jupiter IC line. Most cities in this country of any size are illustrated in my book, *Horoscopes of the Western Hemisphere*, published by ACS in San Diego. Years of research and subsequent observation have convinced me of the validity of the charts given in my book. In a manner of speaking, you will simply have to trust my research, judgment and astrological expertise and rectification methods before you can compare your natal chart to those cities given in my book.

Most astrologers seem to prefer using the incorporation, or charter, date for a community, as it's often the only one available without a great deal of research. Some astrologers, even if investigating a city's history, are not certain as to what constitutes the birth of that particular place. The founding chart of a city or town always takes precedence over an incorporation chart as most cities are chartered years after their initial settlement. The founding chart shows the needs and wants of that city's people and the means by which they will achieve their destiny. The incorporation chart tells me how that city is governed, nothing more. If you'll be working for the government of a specific community, then by all means compare your natal chart to the incorporation chart. But don't fail to also analyze its founding chart which may have an entirely different meaning.

Let's suppose you can't find the founding date of a small town or you're living out in the middle of the country miles from the center of town which has not been chartered, you'll do well to find the date when the county you're living in was created by the state legislature. For suburban areas or unincorporated areas of the larger metropolitan area, I suggest you do a comparison between you and the chart of the chief city in your area. Some large metropolitan areas have more than one major city, like San Francisco, Los Angeles or New York. Find the closest large city to your place of residence or where you want to live and draw up a synastry or composite chart. Those here in southern California should always do a comparison using Los Angeles first, then Long Beach if they live in the southern part of the county near the harbor or Anaheim if they live in Orange County. Those in the San Francisco Bay Area should use San Jose if they live in the southern part or reside in Santa Clara County while those in the East Bay should use Oakland. In my book, *Horoscopes of the Western Hemnishphere*, the charts of over 300 American and Canadian cities are illustrated. Even if you don't completely agree with

my findings as to time or date, I suggest you erect a composite or synastry chart before moving so you can anticipate your reaction to that specific environment. I think you'll be pleasantly surprised, especially if you've already spent some time in that locale.

The composite chart as outlined in Section VII is erected according to your RELOCATED MC, not the one at your birthplace. You must always, repeat ALWAYS, calculate the Composite chart using your relocated MC. Failure to do so will result in a warped interpretation that will make no sense at all. In order for two entities to have the same perspective, they must be in the same place, right? If one person was born in New York and another was born in Chicago, but they meet in Los Angeles, then the composite chart for those two people in Los Angeles is based using their relocated midheavens, not the ones at their place of birth. When that couple journeys to another city, their relationship will change as will their outlook on things. Doing composite charts in this manner quickly illustrates why relationships that thrive in one locale could fall apart when that couple moves to another community. Of course, the planets and the aspects they make to one another will never change, only their house positions and the aspects made to the angles. I've seen hundreds of partnerships which have really terrible aspects between the two individuals, yet for some strange reason, they're still together. What often appears on the surface as possible using the synastry graph in reality often proves to be completely unworkable after the composite chart is erected. You must always do the synastry and composite chart together in order to find if the relationship between you and another entity (person or city) is worth pursuing.

Sections VIII and IX deal with what I call "unseen forces" involving numerology and biorhythms. I don't pretend to understand the occult or esoteric meaning of numbers or biorhythms, but from years of research they both work in a strange manner. For those simply desiring a short-cut and don't want to get involved with the long hours of astrological analysis, these two sections are exactly what they've been looking for. One word of caution, however, when doing numerological evaluations: you must use the full name of a place, not just its "first" name. Failure to do this will result in confusion. Many numerologists disagree with me on this but the proof is in the pudding, so to speak. After all, does one really presume that Springfield, Massachusetts, Ohio, Illinois and Missouri are identical? Failure to use the state along with the city name gives you only half the picture. Biorhythms are fascinating to me and I've worked with them for years. I have no clue whatsoever as to how or why they should work, but then the forces of nature are often not apparent to us ordinary mortals. I use biorhythms and numerology only for the purposes of compatibility, not for analysis of the community.

Each of us at certain times in our lives are drawn to one place over another. This could be due to progressions or major transits affecting the angles of our natal or relocated charts. I strongly advocate looking at progressions and directions with any method outlined in this book. You might find that when your progressed Sun goes over the MC of a particular place that you experience good fortune and honor in that place. But by the time transiting Saturn, for example, hits that point, it's time to retrench or move away to a more liberating environment. Knowing what to expect in advance is one of the major clues of success. If you play the game correctly, you'll be in the right place at the right time and in most instances, be able to have your cake and eat it too.

I firmly believe that it's your God-given right and responsibility to find that place which brings out those qualities you wish to express and where your potential for success and happiness are maximized. It's also your sacred duty to avoid those places that will inhibit your growth, as ignorance of the forces of nature can cost you dearly. As my mother once said - once you've made your bed, you're the one who has to lie in it. No place on earth is completely perfect, but somewhere on this planet is your individual Garden of Eden, your personal Utopia or Nirvana to which you are entitled. I sincerely hope this book enables you to find that particular place

where you can be the Master of your Fate and Captain of your Ship. BON VOYAGE!

Marc Penfield
Hollywood, CA
May 1991

SECTION I

THE RELOCATION CHART

Calculating the relocated chart is as easy as erecting a natal horoscope, but with one major exception. For all relocated charts, you must compute the chart as if you had been born in that locale, thus making the Sidereal Time earlier or later than the Sidereal Time at your birth. For example, if you were born at 11AM in Boston and wish to erect your relocated chart for San Francisco, you must first change the birthtime to 8AM, as San Francisco is on PST, or three hours earlier than Boston, which is on EST. If you wish to move to New York, your birthtime would still be 11AM, but the degree on the MC and ASC would be lower as New York is west of Boston. Best rule of thumb to remember is: moving east, ADD. Moving west, SUBTRACT. To verify exactly which time zone should be used, I suggest you purchase one of the two atlases published by ACS in San Diego as time zones often switch from year to year, not to mention the perpetual confusion over Daylight Savings or Summer Time which occurred prior to 1967 in the USA. Always remember to calculate your birthtime in Standard Time, deducting the hour or two that might have been in effect during the year of your birth.

Another method you can use if you can't figure out the time zone is to calculate the distance of your birthplace from Greenwich and the distance of the place you wish to investigate from Greenwich. The figure will be in hours, minutes and seconds. Subtract the smaller figure from the larger to get the distance in hours, minutes and seconds which you then add or subtract from the sidereal time on your natal horoscope. In countries where time zones are either obscure or absent, I find this the most reliable method to use. For example:

San Francisco	From Greenwich	8hr 09min 40sec
Boston	From Greenwich	4hr 44min 16sec

Difference to be subtracted		3hr 25sec 24sec

Now look up that natal Sidereal Time and subtract the above figure to ascertain the sidereal time of your relocated MC. Now place the remaining house cusps around the wheel, using Porphyry house cusps, or Placidus or Koch if you prefer.

Let's erect the natal chart for Liberace to illustrate the above methods. Liberace was born in West Allis, Wisconsin on May 16, 1919, at 11:15PM CWT. His natal MC is computed as follows:

S.T. at Noon on 5/16/1919	03:32:36
Plus the birthtime	10:15:00
Plus 10 sec. hourly increment	01:14
Plus longitudinal difference from Central Time Zone meridian	08:00
Plus correction for birthplace longitude	00:58

S.T. at birth for Liberace	13:58:15

Looking in *Easy Tables*, this gives a MC of 1 Scorpio 44.

Relocating Liberace's chart to Las Vegas is done as follows:

S.T. at Noon on 5-16-1919	03:32:36
Add the relocated birthtime (You deduct 2 hours as Las Vegas is on PST, two hours behind CST.)	08:15:00
Plus 10 sec. per hour increment	01:21
Difference from the PST meridian	19:24
Correction for longitude	01:16

S.T. for Liberace in Las Vegas	12:09:37

Looking in *Easy Tables*, this gives a MC of 2 Libra 36.

If you prefer to erect the relocated chart by the other method:

Las Vegas is	7hrs 40min 36sec west of Greenwich	
West Allis is	5hrs 52min 00sec west of Greenwich	
	--	
Difference is	1hr 48min 36sec	

which is subtracted from his natal sidereal time at birth.

Liberace's natal S.T. is	13hrs 58min 15sec
Subtract difference	1hr 48min 36sec
S.T. for Las Vegas is	12hrs 09min 39sec

You'll note the difference between the two systems is a mere 2 seconds of sidereal time. I prefer to use the second system as it's much quicker and I don't have to worry about what time zone was in effect.

Throughout this book, I've chosen five famous individuals who made a lasting impression on Las Vegas, or vice versa. The sources for their birth-charts are as follows:

HOWARD HUGHES Born Dec. 24, 1905, at 11PM CST in Houston, TX. Data from his former astrologer to me in 1966.

LIBERACE Born May 16, 1919, at 11:15PM CWT in West Allis, WI. according to his birth certificate.

BUGSY SIEGEL Born Feb. 28, 1906, at 11:22PM EST in New York, NY from Marion Meyer Drew in one of her books.

ROBERT URICH Born Dec. 19, 1946, at 9:40PM EST in Toronto, OH, according to his birth certificate.

KEN USTON Born Jan. 12, 1935, at 3AM EST in New York, NY, per data given to Lois Rodden.

The reason I've chosen Las Vegas, Nevada, to illustrate how relocation works is because its birthdate and birthtime were well recorded in local newspapers and history books. Las Vegas, Nevada, was founded on May 15, 1905 at 10AM PST when an auction began to sell land in this city by the railroad.

All of us know who Howard Hughes was, an eccentric genius who was one of the pioneers of Hollywood during the early days of talkies. Hughes was also an inventor who designed a cantilevered brassiere for Jane Russell as well as the largest airplane ever built, the Spruce Goose. Hughes spent the last years of his life isolated from the outside world in places like Nassau, Las Vegas or Acapulco. He died during a plane trip from Acapulco back to his birthplace in Houston in 1976.

Liberace needs no introduction. Possibly the most flamboyant showman to ever hit Las Vegas, a town used to gaudy displays of opulence, the costumes he wore were studded with gems that would pay for a king's ransom. Liberace never married due to his preference for sexual encounters with members of his own sex and died of AIDS at his home in Palm Springs, California, in 1986.

Bugsy Siegel was an aspiring actor who tried to hit the big time in Hollywood but failed miserably. His earlier years as a mobster and hitman from Brooklyn were unknown to most of the movie world and during World War II he made frequent trips to Las Vegas. Siegel envisioned that desert oasis as a gambling paradise and through mob connections obtained funds to build his dream palace, the Flamingo Hotel and Casino, which opened in 1946.

It was to be the gaudiest and most opulent resort in the country, but after the war, building materials were hard to obtain. Relations with those erecting the hotel proved troublesome: workers often stole material used during the day and sold it back to Siegel the following morning. One person marveled at the huge amount of cement being used to which Siegel replied, "I need a lot. If you don't like it, I'll save a little of it for you." The Flamingo finally opened the day after Christmas 1946 and less than six months later, Siegel was shot in his Beverly Hills home by an assassin.

Robert Urich was a small-time actor who finally hit the big time when he was given the role of a private eye named Dan Tanna in the TV series, *Vegas*. After many years in this role, failing to feel secure or comfortable in Las Vegas, he finally left the west coast and moved to Boston where he filmed another series.

Ken Uston was an executive in a stock brokerage house when in 1973 he began to play blackjack in Las Vegas. Five years later, after winning over $3.5 million, he was banned from this town forever. He had won too much money which made the casino bosses extremely nervous watching their profits go down the drain. Uston was accused of card counting among other things.

READING THE RELOCATED CHART

After erecting your relocated chart, note first the aspects being made to the ASC and MC. Use only a 3-degree orb for the conjunction, sextile, square, trine and inconjunct. You might also want to note the number of semisquares or sesquares, quintiles, septiles or noviles. I don't have enough data from which to draw a firm conclusion as to the effectiveness of the lesser-known aspects so I have eliminated them from Section II of this book.

The next step is to note in which house sits the ruler of the natal ASC. Aspects to that planet will not have changed from the natal chart, only its house position and relation to the angles of the relocated chart. It might also be wise to note the ruler of the relocated ASC as well and to see if there's any relationship between the two. If the natal ASC ruler occupies a house which severely limits its positive expression due to its natal aspect structure, it might be wise to choose another locale where the natal ASC ruler is more beneficially positioned.

Note also whether the rulers of the angles in your natal chart make aspects to the angles in the new relocated chart. I've found that people succeed famously in locales where the rulers of their natal ASC, MC, DESC and IC make aspects to the relocated angles. If the relocated chart also has the Sun or Jupiter aspecting the angle place where prosperity and success are sure to be found in abundance.

Also note which planets are angular in the relocated chart, even if they don't aspect the angles. They will play a strong, but somewhat subordinate role in your life but won't demand or require center stage or the attention like planets conjunct the angles.

If at all possible, try and keep planets out of the sixth, eighth or twelfth houses. Placing planets in these houses is often fraught with danger for those who don't know how to handle the intensity those spheres of activity demand. If you're content to be placed into a subordinate position, then planets in the sixth house might be perfect for you. If you want to escape from pressures of the outside world and love a life of secrecy and privacy, by moving to a place where several planets occupy the twelfth house might be just what is needed for you at this time in your life. The eighth house is always perilous and for those not wishing to experience massive transformation, emotional or physical regeneration, this locale could be like living in hell.

Any house which has more than three planets should be analyzed in depth. Activities represented by that sector of the chart will occupy a considerable portion of your time and effort. For example, if you have a five-planet stellium in the fifth house at birth and move to a place where they now occupy the sixth house, the natural spontaneity and exuberance in the birthplace will largely be absent in the new locale. Your natural love of life and thirst for pleasure still survive, but they will assume a secondary role as work now becomes more important than romance.

Note which houses hold the Sun and Moon. Those needs, wants and desires which occupied your childhood may assume a different focus and your present requirements are likely to be focused on other things.

Watch out for what I call "double aspects," or one planet aspecting two angles in the relocated horoscope. If one of them is a conjunction, that is the most potent one operating: the other aspect assumes a secondary role. For example, Albert Schweitzer had the Sun conjunct the IC in Lambarene, Gabon, where he built a hospital but the Sun was also square the ASC/DESC axis as well. Kaiser Wilhelm had Mars conjunct the MC in Berlin but the planet of war was also trine his ASC to boot. Some astrologers might view both aspects with equal intensity, but from extensive research, the conjunction occupies the throne when "double aspects" like this occurs. When a planet makes an aspect to both angles and a conjunction is not involved, the meaning of both aspects should be considered. One of them will affect your social environment and the manner in which you present yourself while the other relates to career and domestic concerns. Lee Iacocca has Saturn sextile the MC in Detroit but Saturn is also inconjunct the ASC. Whether Saturn operated on a strictly personal level or concentrated its energy on career and domestic matters is a moot point - they both were affected.

If you should send to ACS in San Diego for one of their Astro-Locality maps, please be aware that inconjuncts are not shown on their map, probably as some still consider this to be a minor aspect.

Some people should never move from their birthplace at all, especially if Venus or Jupiter occupy their natal fourth house. When this occurs, however, relocation might be ill-advised unless they were in an occupation that required them to relocate. Malefic influences, especially Saturn or Pluto in the fourth house, make it imperative the individual relocate as soon as possible. Get out of town and the quicker the better for danger lurks in the shadows unless those malefic planets are extremely well-aspected. My sister has Mars and Saturn in the fourth at her birthplace trine the Moon, ruler of the IC. But both planets are square the ASC, which is ruled by Mars. Thus in the Midwest, my sister has the ruler of her ASC and MC in the fourth, square the rising degree but trine to the ruler of the fourth house. She seems to be content to live near her birthplace, but then Aries rising types love challenges more than most people.

If benefic planets are found in the third house, a move to a neighboring city might be suggested. If benefic planets occupy the ninth house, then residence in a foreign country should be contemplated. The reverse is true if malefics occupy those houses.

Always remember to look at the natal chart before you make your final decision, as its imprint on your psyche is permanent, indelible and irrevocable, just like the stamp placed over your passport picture. You're stuck with those influences for the rest of your life, like it or not, and by moving to another locale, you adjust only your focus, the picture remains the same. A person with Mars rising, for example, will always have a tendency to be argumentative, impatient, daring and pushy. Moving that person to a place where Venus now conjuncts the ASC puts a new veneer over the original persona, but the irritable and selfish vibration of Mars lies waiting just beneath the surface. Think of yourself as a beautiful table: by refinishing or polishing it over the years (thru progressions, transits or directions), you've created a slightly different impression which often hides the original material. All the paint and varnish in the world can't cover your basic ingredients. Unless you remember this, you're likely to be disappointed or confused as to why your relocated chart doesn't work as well as you hoped that it would. You always operate within the limitations of the birthchart, only your perspective enlarges or alters when you move to a different location.

ANALYZING THE RELOCATED CHART

The most enigmatic personality of the 20th century, Howard Hughes, was born only 7 months after the city of Las Vegas was founded. Looking at his natal chart, Mercury, ruler of the ASC and MC, is the only planet aspecting his natal angles. Placed in the fourth house, it indicated the introversion for which he was so famous and offers a clue regarding his obsessive need for security and privacy. Relocating his chart to Las Vegas, however, we note that Jupiter (ruler of the natal IC) conjuncts the MC, indicative of real estate speculation and the general good fortune Hughes encountered in this desert city. Mercury, ruler of the natal ASC and MC, makes no

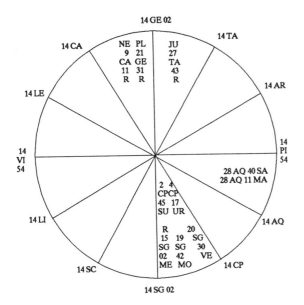

Figure 1. Natal Horoscope for Howard Hughes.

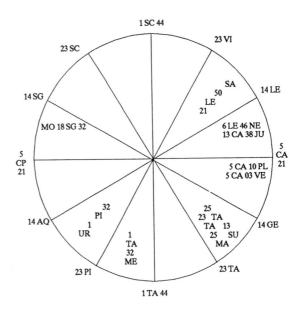

Figure 3. Natal Horoscope for Liberace .

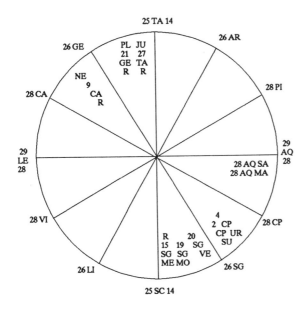

Figure 2. Relocated Horoscope for Howard Hughes.

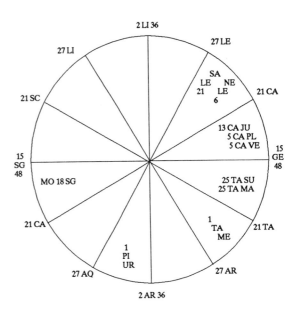

Figure 4. Relocated Horoscope for Liberace .

11

aspects to the relocated angles but the relocated ASC ruler, the Sun, trines the ASC from the fifth house of gambling and speculation. Hughes may have revelled in the attention he received, grabbing the headlines day after day. Mars and Saturn opposite the ASC, or conjunct the DESC, and both square the MC made it difficult for him to associate with outsiders, so he holed himself up like a hermit far from the prying eyes of the public or media. Since Hughes was a Capricorn, he could handle the nature of Saturn much better than those born under other signs. But for most mortals, social interaction is very important to their development as a human being and a requisite for happiness. But then Capricorns often do things the difficult way and seldom shirk from arduous situations. Note that Neptune, ruler of Hughes' natal DESC, semisquares the MC and sesquares the IC. These little used aspects point to the allure and mystery surrounding his whereabouts which were shrouded in secrecy. Hughes was secretive to begin with due to Pluto's opposition to planets in his natal fourth house.

Looking at Liberace's natal chart, we see that Venus and Pluto, rulers of the natal MC and IC, are opposing the Ascendant. This is a difficult situation at best and no doubt influenced his relationship with his parents. Relocation would be advised from this combination of aspects to a place where they would occupy a less prominent position. In Las Vegas, the Venus/Pluto conjunction squares the MC in the seventh house but not in aspect to the ASC. The parental influence would still be strong but without the threat shown in the birth chart. Liberace's earning power was great in Las Vegas due to Uranus, ruler of his natal second house, trine the MC in the second house. His stage presence was bold and gaudy due to the inconjunct of Neptune to the relocated MC. Mercury opposite the natal MC is a good indication of restlessness and desire for movement and with Saturn, ruler of the natal ASC, sesquare the natal ASC and the Moon, ruler of the natal DESC, also semisquare the natal MC, relocation would be strongly advised. Had Liberace remained in the Midwest, his name would never have become a household word.

Relocating Liberace's chart to Las Vegas alters things considerably. The Moon sits on the ASC indicating massive publicity, especially from women for whom he brought out their mothering instincts. Jupiter, ruler of the relocated ASC, inconjuncts the ASC indicating Liberace's tendency for extravagance and his penchant for lavish costumes. His reputation was larger-than-life, his life filled with exuberance and abundance. Mercury and Uranus inconjunct the relocated MC in a Yod made intimate relationships difficult or tenuous as Mercury rules the relocated DESC. Moving Saturn, ruler of the natal ASC, from its sesquare to the natal ASC to a rather wide trine is a decided improvement. Saturn's square to the Sun and Mars does bode a strong health warning as the Sun rules the natal eighth house and squares a planet in that house as well. Liberace died of AIDS, no doubt due to this natal affliction which would be powerful irrespective of where he was living at the time.

Bugsy Siegel's chart is fraught with danger on one hand and indicates great success on the other. The gangster who literally put Las Vegas on the map had no positive aspects to his ASC/DESC axis in this gambling mecca. Mars, co-ruler of his natal ASC, opposes the relocated ASC, so Siegel made many enemies which might have contributed to his assassination. Venus, ruler of his natal DESC, inconjuncts the relocated ASC, so many adjustments had to be made on a continual basis which was difficult for Siegel to comprehend. Mercury and the Moon are also inconjunct the relocated ASC, so life in Las Vegas was hardly a bed of roses, regardless of the publicity he received. Aspects to the MC favor somewhat better, even with the square of Mars to the MC. Despite problems with workers building his dream palace, Siegel managed to pull it off, so in a business sense, career matters progressed better than those on the personal level for Siegel in Las Vegas, due to Mercury aspecting the relocated angles.

Note Siegel's stellium in the relocated fifth house of entertainment, pleasure and gambling. Siegel was a natural in this environment, despite his ties to the mob back in Brooklyn which financed his enter-

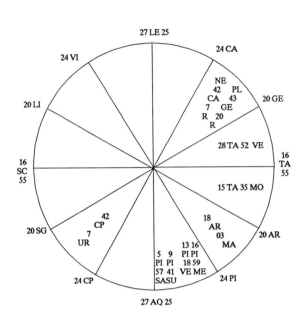

Figure 5. Natal Horoscope for Bugsy Siegel.

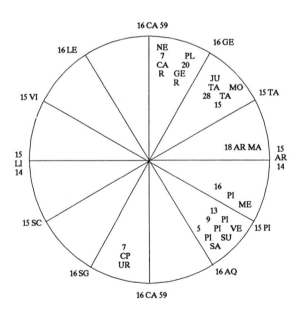

Figure 6. Relocated Horoscope for Bugsy Siegel.

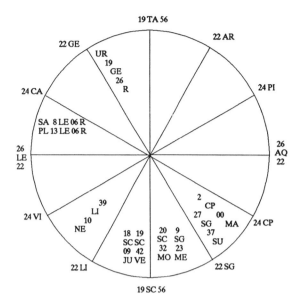

Figure 7. Natal Horoscope for Robert Urich.

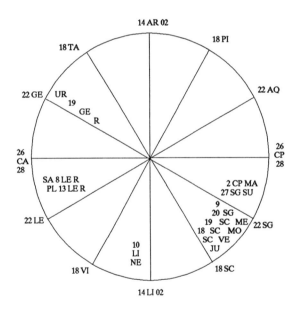

Figure 8. Relocated Horoscope for Robert Urich.

prise. Siegel's vision is shown by Neptune in the ninth opposing Uranus, ruler of the relocated fifth house. Most planets on the west side of the chart put him at the mercy of outside forces he couldn't control, be it the mob or the union workers building his hotel.

Robert Urich's relocated chart shows a dichotomy. Good business sense on one hand combined with domestic confusion and over-assertion of his individuality. Even though he had a hit TV series in this town, he was never really comfortable or secure. Urich felt that Las Vegas was too plastic and transient, too wrapped-up in its own narcissism with few cultural activities which appealed to his sense of refinement. Urich is a strong family man who is much more sensitive and emotional than is apparent from the macho types he portrays on screen. Stress and tension on the personal level are shown by the Sun, ruler of the natal ASC, inconjunct the relocated ASC. Domestic impermanence is shown by Neptune in opposition to the MC, or conjunct the IC.

If Urich's birthtime is four minutes off, Neptune's aspect would be within my accepted orb of 3 degrees. Neptune conjunct the IC gives the individual little feeling of being rooted: something always comes up which pulls the rug out from under you. Pluto, ruler of his natal IC, trines the relocated MC but sits in the first house widely conjunct Saturn. Las Vegas put more stress on Urich than he cared to admit, and from his natal chart, he should have stayed close to his birthplace due to Venus and Jupiter conjunct his natal IC.

But when you're an actor, you go where the jobs are, having little choice in the matter. Urich's natal ASC ruler, the Sun, trines the ASC at birth. Having Saturn and Pluto in the twelfth natally is considerably better than placing them into the first house where their negative tendencies are brought out into the forefront, opening a can of worms and exposing skeletons in the closet. Clearly, Urich was happier in Boston which is close to his birthplace than he ever was in Las Vegas or Hollywood.

Ken Uston has a different story to tell about the gaudiest city on earth. Being ousted from the casinos after winning over $3.5 million in five years, he was a *persona non grata*, someone who beat the odds in a town where everyone loves a winner except those running the place. Note that Pluto, ruler of his natal ASC, conjuncts the relocated MC, and true to the nature of that "undercover" planet, Uston's method of winning was obscured in secrecy. Saturn, ruler of the relocated IC, inconjuncts the MC showing the driving ambition which led to his downfall. Venus, ruler of the natal DESC and the relocated ASC, makes no aspects whatsoever to the relocated chart. Uston would thus have a hard time relating to outsiders or strangers or in handling any opposition that came his way. Note that the Sun squares the relocated ASC and opposes the MC, clearly indicative of the massive ego trip that played a major role in Uston's quest to beat the system. His sojourn in Las Vegas was no doubt a personal one, motivated not only for money, but for power and glory as well.

The Moon, ruler of his relocated MC, squares the MC and conjuncts Uranus indicating his unpopularity with his "employers," those managers who ran the casinos he took for broke. Having the Sun conjunct the IC, however, made Uston feel like he was at home here in a town where excitement and danger lurked around every corner and the big win was always imminent. Uston's T-square was activated to such a degree in Las Vegas that he over estimated his own abilities. Being a Scorpio rising at birth, Uston loved to "push the envelope" and his Moon in Aries loved the challenge of being the first to burn and conquer, and then move on to more uncharted pastures.

From the foregoing examples, it appears that most people do best in a place where the ruler of one of their natal angles aspects one of the relocated angles. If the aspect is positive, then success and good fortune are promised, either on the personal or professional level. If the aspects are negative, however, conditions in that locale are inimical to one's peace of mind and life is simply a struggle to survive. You're often placed at the mercy of the elements you can neither control nor comprehend.

Now it's time to look at your relocated map to ascertain those places where the rulers of your natal angles are in aspect to the relocated MC and ASC. Highlight these lines with a marking pen, doing the same for any Sun or Jupiter line in the vicinity. Then if you're in an ambitious mood, erect a chart for each place along those lines that initially appeal to you. You'll be surprised that many cities you may never have considered could be quite beneficial to your development or destiny, while others which have occupied your attention over the years seem to offer little satisfaction or possibility for success in business, love and romance or happiness in general.

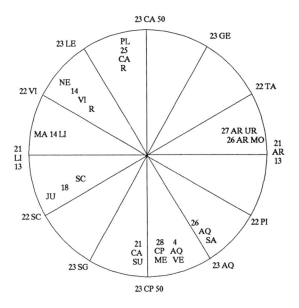

Figure 10. Relocated Horoscope for **Ken Uston.**

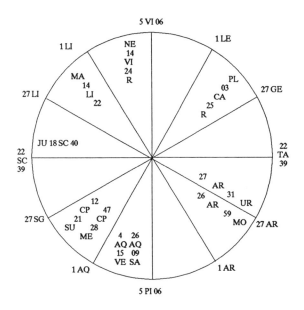

Figure 9. Natal Horoscope for **Ken Uston.**

SECTION II

ASPECTS TO THE ASCENDANT AND MID-HEAVEN

Please note: Before you read this section trying to find which aspects are operating in your projected place of residence, it might be wise to note those aspects to your natal ASC and MC as well. Those influences are impossible to eradicate and will be firmly embedded in your psyche from the moment of your birth. To assume that you can eliminate factors relating to your early environment or genetic structure is not only stupid but fallacious. To paraphrase Abraham Lincoln: "you can fool some of the people some of the time, some of the people all of the time but you can't fool all of the people all of the time." To do the above, the only person you'll be fooling will be yourself.

NATURE OF THE ASPECTS (Using only a 3-degree orb)

CONJUNCTIONS
- the most powerful aspect one can have in any chart
- similar to Aries
- highly energetic, impatient, intense, magnetic and compelling
- capacity to alter one's lifestyle, perception and feelings
- native identifies with the planet involved
- assumes a new identity constructive or destructive
- positive or negative manifestation

SEXTILES
- brings out the best of both planets
- works for the common good of each similar to Gemini or Aquarius
- communicative and socially oriented capacity for friendship and cooperation
- brings good fortune and opportunities for advancement
- participation in group activities
- social acceptance and ability to influence the public

SQUARES
- difficulties requiring challenge, motivation and assertion
- similar to Cancer and Capricorn
- conflicts with those in authority
- obstacles and barriers placed in the path of ambition or contentment
- frustrations can arise when one refuses to bend or adjust
- tension and disruption due to personal limitations or understanding

TRINES
- an easy or lazy aspect requiring motivation in order to manifest
- similar to Leo and Sagittarius
- highly creative and inspirational
- latent talents and abilities used with little effort
- balance and support from the public
- good will and benevolence
- desire to conserve energy
- matters remain static and unchanged

INCONJUNCTS
- a difficult aspect which acts like a warning light
- similar to Virgo and Scorpio
- analytical, critical and intense
- the "flies in the ointment" which gum up an organism or machine
- snags and predicaments which deter us from our original plan
- quandaries resulting in indecision or anxiety
- health problems
- over compensates through extravagance to counter basic deficiencies

OPPOSITIONS
- qualities within us that we expect others to fulfill
- similar to Libra
- cooperative and unifying or a conflict of wills
- complementary or opposite characteristics which remain dormant
- capacity for understanding and awareness or separation and antagonism
- battle for power and control
- polarization of understanding

SEMISQUARE and SESQUARE (not used in this book)
- fixity and rigidity which precludes total understanding
- minor irritations and annoyances
- like the itch that won't go away
- capacity for analysis or dissection
- highly critical and purgative
- tenacious and stubborn insistence on keeping the status quo

NATURE OF THE PLANETS

THE SUN
- personal identity
- how one's individual is expressed
- courage and vitality, authority and leadership ability
- self-confidence, will-power and creative instincts
- ability to give and receive love and affection
- desire for prominence and attention

THE MOON
- relationships with women and the public in general
- desire for security and domestic harmony
- general lifestyle and habit patterns
- restlessness and capacity for change
- feelings and emotions

MERCURY
- communicative ability and desire to be understood
- capacity to be logical, sensible and rational
- opportunity for study and attention to detail
- need for change and variety
- ability to find work and employment

VENUS
- personal gratification through intimate relationships
- social activities and romantic encounters
- desire for companionship
- ability to make commitments
- artistic or cultural opportunities and abilities
- acceptance by the social set

- manners and etiquette
- self-indulgence in food or pleasure-seeking

MARS
- constructive or destructive expenditure of energy
- temper and passion
- jealousy or possessiveness
- conflict and violence
- one's assertion of authority
- pioneering instincts and desire for independence
- confrontations with the police
- contacts with the military

JUPITER
- expansion of consciousness
- interest in religion or philosophy
- cooperation from those in superior positions
- possible wasting of energy or talent
- self indulgence or extravagance
- success, honor and good fortune with little effort
- personal morality and ethical standards

SATURN
- need for discipline and structure
- capacity for organization
- personal deficiencies, limitations or restrictions
- basic lessons needed for survival, autonomy and self-sufficiency
- degree of ambition
- ability to relate to those in authority
- business or political aspirations
- long-term progress comes through patience and diligence

URANUS
- compulsive need for freedom and independence
- sudden and unexpected occurrences which upset the daily routine
- willingness to work for the common good
- clubs or organizations
- weird or eccentric behavior which is "out of sync"
- scientific or technological interests
- creative originality
- pioneering spirit which lights the path for others to follow

18

NEPTUNE
- where we experience deceit, confusion, dejection and rejection
- idol-worship and idealism
- seeing life through rose-colored glasses
- capacity for compassion and understanding
- the need for sacrifice
- vulnerability and impressionability
- where one is most gullible
- fantasy and illusion hard to separate from fact and reality
- escapist tendencies
- alcohol and drug abuse
- those living on welfare or in hospitals, asylums or prisons

PLUTO
- the need for massive regeneration and personal transformation
- superior will needed for control and manipulation of the environment
- power and coercion
- force and intimidation
- involvement with criminals
- where life is purged and laid waste and thus cleansed for the future
- capacity to bend to the will of the public
- strong political bent
- irrevocable and intense
- compelling and dangerous
- life threatening
- high degree of magnetism and charisma
- ability to influence the masses
- constant peril from unstable and violent elements in our society

SUN CONJUNCT ASC
- where you're noticed for your impressive personality or dramatic appearance
- few can ignore the impact of your regal bearing
- an overwhelming abundance of personal magnetism and charisma
- a tendency to dominate people or situations
- where one puts up a good front and seeks the limelight
- often a show-off due to abundant self-confidence

- where one requires abundant admiration and respect as well as love and affection
- where your cheerful and sunny disposition desires to hold center stage
- you desire to be a person of importance and authority
- highly creative, overly generous and benevolent to those less fortunate

Prince Albert in London
Fatty Arbuckle in Hollywood
Augustus Caesar in Rome
Boris Becker in London
Wm. Gladstone in London
Merv Griffin in Hollywood
U.S. Grant in Vicksburg
Charlton Heston in Hollywood
Abraham Lincoln in Washington
Mao Tse Tung in Peking
Groucho Marx in Hollywood
Nero in Rome
Pat Nixon in Washington
H. Ross Perot in Dallas
Leontyne Price in New York
Queen Victoria in London
Orson Welles in Hollywood
Duchess of Windsor in London
Yogananda in Hollywood

SUN SEXTILE ASC
- easy to make important social contacts with people of influence
- where you project a positive attitude which gains recognition
- success in field of communications
- good for writers and journalists
- power and authority through clubs or group activities
- considerable charm and popularity wins others to your viewpoint
- where you want to be constantly on the go
- very restless due to stimulating and exciting environment
- wants to be where the action is
- many opportunities to expand one's consciousness or understanding
- where one's creativity is recognized

- highly inventive and original
- sometimes flighty and superficial
- your mind wanders from subject to subject

Konrad Adenauer in Bonn
Jim Bakker in Charlotte
Helena Blavatsky in London
Lizzie Borden in Fall River
Father Damien in Hawaii
Thomas Edison in Menlo Park
Harrison Ford in Hollywood
Greta Garbo in Hollywood
Antonio Gaudi in Barcelona
Hermann Goering in Berlin
John Paul I in Rome
Charles Lindbergh in New York
Louis XIV in Paris
Marilyn Monroe in Hollywood
J. P. Morgan in New York
Rupert Murdoch in New York
Napoleon I in Paris
Auguste Rodin in Paris
Eleanor Roosevelt in Washington

Eamon de Valera in Dublin
Christian Dior in Paris
Zsa Zsa Gabor in Hollywood
Paul Gauguin in Tahiti
Ava Gardner in Hollywood
Martin Luther in Wittenberg
Karl Marx in London
Joe Montana in San Francisco
Michelangelo in Rome
Richard Nixon in Washington
Nostradamus in Paris
Paul VI in Rome
Nancy Reagan in Washington
Oral Roberts in Tulsa
J. D. Rockefeller in Cleveland
Nelson Rockefeller in Washington
Artur Rubinstein in New York
Lillian Russell in New York
Carl Sandburg in Chicago
Albert Schweitzer in Gabon
P. B. Shelley in Italy
Woodrow Wilson in Washington

SUN SQUARE ASC
- where conflict exists between the way you project yourself and how others view you
- conflicts with authority figures, especially males
- where you try to dominate situations and people
- overbearing manner refuses to take a back seat
- your ego needs continual reinforcement and support
- need to prove yourself causes tension in relationships
- self-confidence is questioned and authority undermined
- pushy and arrogant sometimes coming off as a real "know it all"
- brags and boasts of one's accomplishments
- an attention grabber who refuses to let others occupy the limelight

Honore de Balzac in Paris
Neville Chamberlain in Munich
Richard Chamberlain in London
Charles Darwin in the Galapagos
John De Lorean in Detroit

SUN TRINE ASC
- where your abundant self-confidence gets results with little effort
- projects a positive attitude with loads of optimism
- where life is lived to the fullest
- often the center of attention
- likes to party and enjoys the social scene
- highly creative and inventive
- always original and compelling
- often self-indulgent with food or sex
- possible weight gain or sexual promiscuity
- strong physical constitution and considerable vitality
- strong willpower inspires others to reach their potential
- nothing is done in half measures, it's all or nothing
- where your individuality is respected and admired by others
- where you need much love, affection, adulation and respect

Simon Bolivar in Caracas
Martin Bormann in Berlin
Coco Chanel in Paris
Deng Xiao Ping in Peking
Frederick the Great in Berlin
Hugh Hefner in Hollywood
Nikita Khrushchev in Moscow
Henry Kissinger in Washington
Lafayette in Philadelphia
Peter Max in New York
A. S. McPherson in Los Angeles
Christina Onassis in Greece
Peter the Great in Leningrad
Dan Quayle in Washington
Gloria Swanson in Hollywood
Giuseppe Verdi in Milan

SUN INCONJUNCT ASC
- where inner conflict requires you to act in a manner foreign to your nature
- sacrifices necessary to accomplish one's aims or ambitions
- possible health problems
- involved with the medical world
- seldom sure others like you for who you really are
- often feels nobody is paying attention to you
- where you must pay more than average attention to details
- overly critical and a perfectionist
- often has a negative outlook on life
- must help others on their road to success
- one's ego must be sublimated
- intense inner turmoil and anxiety
- often worries about the impression one makes on others

Josephine Baker in Paris
Beethoven in Vienna
Anita Bryant in Miami
Pablo Casals in San Juan
Tom Dooley in Laos
Bette Davis in Hollywood
Mary Baker Eddy in Boston
D. D. Eisenhower in Washington
Galileo in Rome
Franz Joseph Haydn in Vienna

Reinhard Heydrich in Berlin
Ivan the Terrible in Moscow
Helen Keller in New York
Nelson Mandela in Johannesburg
Maximilian in Mexico
Harvey Milk in San Francisco
Ronald Reagan in Washington
Adlai Stevenson in New York
Shirley Temple in Hollywood
Duke of Windsor in London

SUN OPPOSITE ASC/CONJUNCT DESC
- success comes through partnerships and relations with the public
- great need to be with someone special
- good for marriage
- others reinforce your ego and sense of self-worth
- wants to shine with others but wants the partner to shine as well
- conflict arises when one refuses to take second place
- egos are often bruised
- vain and ambitious for social success
- overly generous and outgoing
- great personal magnetism
- where one puts one's lover on a pedestal
- often idealizes romance
- strong bond of mutual attraction
- passionate with partners
- often seeks to control or manipulate others by dominating their every move

Gloria Allred in Los Angeles
Helena Blavatsky in New York
Charles de Gaulle in Paris
Jean Harlow in Hollywood
Joan of Arc in Rouen
J. F. Kennedy in London
Nikolai Lenin in Zurich
Billy Martin in New York
Bette Midler in Hollywood
Father Serra in California
Joseph Smith in Nauvoo

SUN CONJUNCT MC
- possibility of fame and renown
- authority and ambition come easily

- often known as a father figure
- aura of superiority and self-confidence
- social success furthers one's professional ambitions
- prefers to be the boss
- finds it difficult to take orders
- radiates an inner glow from a positive attitude and sunny disposition
- often explodes in fury or anger when one's authority is questioned
- attracted to masculine things and ideals
- often a hero worshiper
- high degree of creativity
- loves to occupy center stage
- great personal magnetism and charisma
- often domineering and bossy
- sometimes dogmatic and insensitive
- seeks quality rather than quality
- wants to live in the grand style

Charles Chaplin in Hollywood
Jerry Falwell in Lynchburg
Frederick the Great in Berlin
Goethe in Weimar
Charles Gordon in the Sudan
W. G. Harding in San Francisco
Alfred Hitchcock in Hollywood
John Paul II in Rome
Juan Carlos in Madrid
R. F. Kennedy in Los Angeles
Martin Luther King in Atlanta
Josef Mengele in Auschwitz
Joe Montana in San Francisco
Napoleon I in Cairo
Nicholas II in Leningrad
Nostradamus in Paris
Jacqueline Onassis in Dallas
Pius XII in Rome
Nancy Reagan in Washington
Ronald Reagan in Hollywood
Nelson Rockefeller in Washington
Albert Speer in Berlin
Elizabeth Taylor in Hollywood

SUN SEXTILE MC
- where one's individuality is easily projected
- advancement comes with ease

- where one takes steps necessary to insure success and good fortune
- sunny disposition appeals to those in power and authority
- social contacts aid one's professional status
- highly independent but has little need to dominate others
- often a role model for others who follow your lead
- tries to do the best job possible
- ambitious and determined
- won't occupy center stage unless one feels they deserve it
- happy and contented in one's career
- many opportunities for overall success and recognition

Boris Becker in London
Anita Bryant in Miami
Jimmy Carter in Washington
Edgar Cayce in Virginia Beach
Coco Chanel in Paris
Charles de Gaulle in Paris
Douglas Fairbanks in Hollywood
Franz Ferdinand in Sarajevo
M. K. Gandhi in New Delhi
Ava Gardner in Hollywood
Bob Geldof in Ethiopia
George Gershwin in Hollywood
Mel Gibson in Sydney
Arthur Godfrey in Miami
Franz Joseph Haydn in Vienna
Aldous Huxley in Hollywood
Joan of Arc in Rouen
Joseph McCarthy in Washington
Prince Philip in London
Knute Rockne in South Bend
Joseph Stalin in Moscow
Dan White in San Francisco

SUN SQUARE MC
- confrontations with those in power and authority
- insists on being first
- thinks one is always right
- refuses to relinquish privileges or to sublimate one's ego

- difficulty cooperating
- prefers to do things your way or not at all
- strong need to control others
- always projects an air of authority
- often domineering, selfish and overly aggressive
- pushes too hard for success
- ambition is often unrealistic
- hard to accept direction from others
- sometimes arrogant or conceited
- ego gets in the way of progress
- always an inner anxiety about one's image or reputation

Fatty Arbuckle in Hollywood
Amelia Earhart on Howland Island
Mary Baker Eddy in Boston
Sigmund Freud in Vienna
U. S. Grant in Washington
Dag Hammarksjold in New York
Jean Harlow in Hollywood
Charlton Heston in Hollywood
Ivan the Terrible in Moscow
Bruce Jenner in Montreal
Helmut Kohl in Bonn
G. Gordon Liddy in Washington
Louis XVI in Paris
Groucho Marx in Hollywood
Pat Nixon in Washington
Carroll Righter in Hollywood
Roman Polanski in Hollywood
Toulouse Lautrec in Paris
Ted Turner in Hollywood
Mark Twain in Hartford
Rudolph Valentino in Hollywood
Barbara Walters in New York

SUN TRINE MC

- personal success in one's profession
- authority is granted with ease
- domestic felicity and harmony
- love and affection in one's home
- tries to create happiness and sunshine
- inspires others to better themselves
- always projects a positive image
- has a well-balanced ego
- has a good opinion of oneself
- has little need for competition

- a great thirst for life
- wants to live in the grand style
- strong creative drive
- good for actors or politicians
- self-confident without being arrogant
- little need to prove oneself
- highly independent but willing to take direction from others
- often lazy preferring to play rather than work
- loves the social scene and nightlife

Jane Addams in Chicago
Rosa Bonheur in Paris
Johannes Brahms in Vienna
H. G. Brown in New York
Joan Crawford in Hollywood
Hermann Goering in Berlin
Che Guevara in Havana
Ethel Kennedy in Washington
J. F. Kennedy in London
Ted Kennedy in Washington
Nikolai Lenin in Leningrad
Mary I in London
Mies van der Rohe in Chicago
Francois Mitterand in Paris
Mozart in Vienna
Meryl Streep in Hollywood
Arturo Toscanini in New York
Giuseppe Verdi in Milan
Queen Victoria in London
Joseph Wambaugh in Los Angeles
Oscar Wilde in Paris
F. L. Wright in Chicago

SUN INCONJUNCT MC

- has difficulty making up one's mind with respect to the career
- matters come up which deter you from your original plan
- many sacrifices needed
- individuality placed on the back burner
- often feels like a pawn or at the mercy of others
- authority figures try to control and manipulate you
- caught up in everyday details
- fails to see the big picture
- life often goes from one extreme to the other

- ambition wavers constantly
- conflict between ambition and apathy
- often a serious attitude about life
- seems to prefer being alone as much as possible

Simon Bolivar in Caracas
Carol Burnett in Hollywood
Richard Burton in Hollywood
Neville Chamberlain in Munich
Father Damien in Hawaii
Eamon de Valera in Dublin
Diane von Furstenburg in New York
Jackie Gleason in Miami
Victor Hugo in Paris
Anver Joffrey in New York
Nehru in New Delhi
William Penn in Philadelphia
Robespierre in Paris
Diana Ross in Detroit
Gloria Steinem in New York
Tina Turner in Dallas
Duke of Windsor in London

SUN OPPOSITE MC/CONJUNCT IC
- one's domestic environment assumes prime importance
- content to live in a world of one's own making
- could become a hermit or social outcast
- good place for retirement
- much stability and security
- needs space and freedom
- hates to live in cramped quarters
- gives much thought to one's inner life
- delves into the subconscious
- often involved with the occult or supernatural
- highly psychic or intuitive
- desires an ideal domestic life with as little tension or stress as possible
- often dependent on others for survival
- often yields to those in authority
- nurturing instinct desires to take care of those less fortunate

Helena Blavatsky in London
Eva Braun in Berlin
Sir Richard Burton in Mecca
Carol Channing in New York

Charles Darwin in the Galapagos
John Dillinger in Chicago
D. D. Eisenhower in London
Ava Gardner in London
Paul Gauguin in Tahiti
Herbert Hoover in Washington
L. Ron Hubbard in Los Angeles
Jim Jones in Guyana
Stacy Keach in London
Douglas MacArthur in Manila
Peter the Great in Leningrad
Pablo Picasso in Paris
Mary Pickford in Hollywood
Bishop Pike in Israel
Lillian Russell in New York
Carl Sandburg in Chicago
Norman Schwarzkopf in Kuwait
Frank Sinatra in Hollywood
Woodrow Wilson in Washington

MOON CONJUNCT ASC
- highly emotional and imaginative
- difficult to hide feelings
- quite changeable and moody
- very restless and indecisive
- intuitive and psychic nature makes one sensitive to the environment
- needs much love and attention
- hates to live alone, always needs company
- relates well to women
- strong maternal instincts
- wants stability and security
- often receives publicity or notoriety
- over indulgence in food or romance
- could have problems with weight
- needs social acceptance but shyness often prevents intimacy
- conventional nature
- goes along with the crowd

Fatty Arbuckle in Hollywood
E. B. Browning in Florence
Jane Fonda in Hanoi
Rajiv Gandhi in New Delhi
Alfred Hitchcock in Hollywood
The Shah in Teheran
Mark Spitz in Munich

Leon Trotsky in Leningrad
Queen Victoria in London

MOON SEXTILE ASC
- peaceful and harmonious domestic environment
- favorable relations with women
- works well with the public
- friends assist in times of crisis and lend emotional or financial support
- social life very important
- finds it hard to be left alone
- attracts conservative, family oriented people
- considerable restlessness causes many changes of job or residence
- possibility of publicity or notoriety
- easily influenced by others
- generally easy going and relaxed with well balanced emotions
- hospitable and sympathetic to those in need

Prince Albert in London
Gloria Allred in Los Angeles
Anita Bryant in Miami
Capt. Cook in Sydney
Calvin Coolidge in Washington
Charles Darwin in the Galapagos
James Dean in Hollywood
John Dillinger in Chicago
Bob Fosse in New York
Harrison Ford in Hollywood
John Holmes in Hollywood
Lady Bird Johnson in Washington
Jim Jones in Guyana
Christine Jorgensen in Denmark
Juan Carlos in Madrid
Sophia Loren in Paris
Louis XVI in Paris
Sir Thomas More in London
Jacqueline Onassis in Greece
Ronald Reagan in Washington
Robespierre in Paris
George Sand in Paris
P. B. Shelley in Italy
Gertrude Stein in Paris
John Sutter in Sacramento
Gloria Swanson in Hollywood
Tina Turner in Dallas

Duke of Wellington at Waterloo
Stanford White in New York
Woodrow Wilson in Washington

MOON SQUARE ASC
- rapid mood swings
- usually overreacts
- never certain from one moment to the next what one's mood will be
- hypersensitive and overly emotional
- conflict between professional and domestic concerns
- restlessness causes frequent changes of jobs and homes
- seldom satisfied with the status quo
- easily annoyed or irritated
- ingrained habit patterns are hard to break
- conflicts within the family
- little understanding of public needs
- disagreements with women and unsympathetic to women's issues
- little real security or stability
- life is like a roller coaster
- many ups and downs

Jane Addams in Chicago
Warren Beatty in Hollywood
A. G. Bell in Boston
Carol Burnett in Hollywood
Charles Chaplin in Hollywood
Chiang Kaishek in Taiwan
Bob Geldof in Ethiopia
Rock Hudson in Hollywood
Anver Joffrey in New York
Nikolai Lenin in Zurich
Karl Marx in London
Mozart in Vienna
Roman Polanski in Hollywood
Mme de Pompadour in Paris
Richard Wagner in Zurich

MOON TRINE ASC
- emotions are well-balanced and flow freely
- appreciated by the public
- the perfect host or hostess
- social life agreeable
- comfortable with all types of people

- pleasant domestic scene
- harmonious family relations
- wants to belong and hates to be left alone
- strong creative impulses
- overly active imagination
- positive attitude gets beneficial results and support
- easily influenced by women
- strong maternal instincts

Roseanne Barr in Hollywood
Boris Becker in London
David Ben Gurion in Jerusalem
William Bligh in Tahiti
Johannes Brahms in Vienna
Mother Cabrini in New York
Fidel Castro in Havana
Eamon de Valera in Dublin
Tom Dooley in Laos
Eugenie in Paris
Jane Fonda in Hollywood
Ernest Hemingway in Havana
Christopher Isherwood in Berlin
Ivan the Terrible in Moscow
Ted Kennedy in Washington
John McEnroe in London
Mata Hari in Paris
Edward R. Murrow in London
Richard Nixon in Washington
Carl Sandburg in Chicago

MOON INCONJUNCT ASC
- one emotional crisis after another
- intense and dramatic outbursts
- emotions must be put on hold until the situation has cleared up
- tendency to criticize causes domestic squabbles and unpopularity
- often projects the exact opposite of what one is really feeling
- periodic explosions of rage or frenzy throws caution to the winds
- attracts people who have difficulty with their emotions
- natural nurturing instincts often suppressed or denied
- runs one's home like a dictator

- very efficient and organized

Jim Bakker in Charlotte
Beethoven in Vienna
Melvin Belli in San Francisco
Bette Davis in Hollywood
Douglas Fairbanks in Hollywood
Bobby Fischer in Iceland
Clark Gable in Hollywood
J. A. Garfield in Washington
J. P. Getty in London
Leona Helmsley in New York
F. de Lesseps in Egypt
Billy Martin in New York
Bette Midler in Hollywood
Rupert Murdoch in New York
Nicholas II in Leningrad
Christina Onassis in Greece
Joseph Smith in Nauvoo
Steven Spielberg in Hollywood
Johann Strauss in Vienna
Elizabeth Taylor in Hollywood
Simon Wiesenthal in Vienna

MOON OPP ASC/CONJUNCT DESC
- very involved with others and the general public
- a follower rather than a leader
- others often sap one's emotions
- highly psychic and intuitive
- expected to play the role of a parent
- the regular "mother hen" type
- interferes or meddles in the affairs of others
- continually seeks advice from women
- marital life filled with many emotional scenes
- prefers to be passive and unobtrusive
- great sensitivity to those less fortunate

Brigitte Bardot in Paris
Betty Ford in Washington
Gerald Ford in Washington
Paul Gauguin in Tahiti
George V in London
Rudolf Hess in Berlin
Hindenburg in Berlin
Grace Kelly in Hollywood
Maria Theresa in Vienna
J.K. Polk in Washington

Albert Schweitzer in Gabon
Grace Slick in San Francisco
Barbra Streisand in Hollywood

MOON CONJUNCT MC

- much popularity and public exposure
- life is an open book
- impossible to remain obscure or anonymous
- every move is noticed
- needs to be with people
- works for the public and intuitive about their needs
- your boss considers you part of their family
- women exert a strong influence
- domestic life is important
- emphasis on stability and security
- often goes overboard providing for the family
- cares for the sick and needy
- strong need for social acceptance
- works well with community organizations
- work might involve food, clothing or shelter
- salespersons do good here
- sentimental, impressionable and changeable
- highly romantic and emotional

John Barrymore in Hollywood
Wm. J. Bryan in Washington
Pearl Buck in Nanking
C. B. DeMille in Hollywood
Deng Xiaoping in Peking
Phil Donahue in Hollywood
Albert Einstein in Princeton
Galileo in Florence
Bob Geldof in Ethiopia
Christopher Isherwood in Berlin
John Paul II in Rome
Ethel Kennedy in Washington
Charles Lindbergh in Paris
Rudolph Nureyev in New York
Yoko Ono in New York
Father Serra in San Diego
Wm. H. Taft in Washington

MOON SEXTILE MC

- great range of influence, especially with women
- well-balanced emotions
- sensitive to the needs of the public

- many opportunities for expression
- publicity and renown
- social life appealing and fortuitous
- handles divergent groups with ease
- domestic scene harmonious
- relations with superiors excellent
- flexible and adaptable
- natural restlessness causes frequent change
- always seeking the ideal job or home
- strong need for security
- desires to care for others
- much sympathy or compassion

Josephine Baker in Paris
Jim Bakker in Charlotte
Lucille Ball in Hollywood
Boris Becker in London
Helena Blavatsky in New York
Cher in Hollywood
Winston Churchill in London
F .F. Coppola in Hollywood
Mme du Barry in Paris
Bobby Fischer in Iceland
M. K. Gandhi in Johannesburg
J. A. Garfield in Washington
Jackie Gleason in Miami
Dag Hammarksjold in New York
Hugh Hefner in Hollywood
Rudolf Hess in Berlin
Ivan the Terrible in Moscow
M. L. King in Memphis
James Madison in Washington
Maria Theresa in Vienna
Mary I in London
Nero in Rome
Pat Nixon in Washington
Aristotle Onassis in Buenos Aires
Lee Harvey Oswald in Dallas
Gavrilo Princip in Sarajevo
Ted Turner in Hollywood
Vincent van Gogh in Arles
Simon Wiesenthal in Vienna
Brigham Young in Salt Lake City

MOON SQUARE MC

- difficult relations with women due to lack of understanding of their needs

- conflict with the mother and family due to lack of patience
- battle between domestic and professional responsibilities
- often unreliable or unpopular due to being "out of sync" with needs of the general populace
- old habits hard to break
- many domestic squabbles or tantrums
- much stress and tension
- frequently flies off the handle
- emotions run contrary to what is expected
- little things upset the balance
- many changes of career due to vacillation or indecision
- cooperation difficult
- prefers to be left alone
- unsatisfactory social life due to basic lack of sympathy or compassion
- one crisis after another
- many ups and downs

Fatty Arbuckle in Hollywood
F. A. Bartholdi in New York
John Belushi in Hollywood
E. B. Browning in Florence
Yul Brynner in Hollywood
Catherine de Medici in Paris
Joan Crawford in Hollywood
D. D. Eisenhower in Washington
Mamie Eisenhower in Washington
Jane Fonda in Hanoi
Rajiv Gandhi in New Delhi
Paul Gauguin in Tahiti
George V in London
John Paul I in Rome
Stacy Keach in London
Grace Kelly in Hollywood
John Lennon in New York
A. S. McPherson in Los Angeles
Machiavelli in Florence
Juan Peron in Buenos Aires
Albert Schweitzer in Gabon
Grace Slick in San Francisco
Mark Twain in San Francisco
Duke of Windsor in London
Duchess of Windsor in London

MOON TRINE MC
- success comes from working with and for the public and their needs
- excels in fields such as acting, sales or politics
- real estate favored
- relations with authority figures favored as you fulfill their demands promptly
- homelife and marriage prosper
- much stability and security
- caring and supportive
- collects the strays of the world
- highly nurturing and overly protective of people and things
- difficult to let go of the past
- good relations with women
- great popularity and favorable publicity

Konrad Adenauer in Bonn
Christian Barnard in Cape Town
Michael Bennett in New York
Barbara Bush in Washington
John Fremont in San Francisco
Joseph Goebbels in Berlin
Francisco Goya in Madrid
Cary Grant in Hollywood
Ernest Hemingway in Idaho
Hindenburg in Berlin
Janis Joplin in San Francisco
Christine Jorgensen in Denmark
Michael Landon in Hollywood
Sophia Loren in Paris
Marie Antoinette in Paris
Jacqueline Onassis in Washington
H. Ross Perot in Dallas
Carroll Righter in Hollywood
Babe Ruth in New York
Diana Spencer in London
Elizabeth Taylor in Rome
Leon Trotsky in Leningrad
Rudolph Valentino in Hollywood
Queen Victoria in London
Lech Walesa in Danzig
William of Orange in London

MOON INCONJUNCT MC
- continual conflict between professional and domestic issues

- sacrifice needed to insure success
- need to set priorities early
- prone to change jobs frequently
- always seeking the ideal
- often pulled in two directions at once
- continual emotional tugs of war
- much confusion and delusion with little stability or security
- difficulty relating to the public
- feels emotionally isolated
- unpopular due to emotional excess
- often plays the role of a martyr
- very misunderstood
- often ignores the larger issues but a personal crusader for the downtrodden

Queen Anne in London
Honore de Balzac in Paris
William Bligh in Tahiti
Anita Bryant in Miami
Joan Collins in Hollywood
John DeLorean in Detroit
John Dillinger in Chicago
Ernest Hemingway in Havana
Reinhard Heydrich in Berlin
Aldous Huxley in Hollywood
Rudyard Kipling in London
Lafayette in Philadelphia
Nikolai Lenin in Leningrad
Karl Marx in London
Harvey Milk in San Francisco
Napoleon I in Moscow
Paul Newman in Hollywood
Manuel Noriega in Panama City
Paul VI in Rome
Bhagwan Rajneesh in Oregon
J. D. Rockefeller in Cleveland
Carl Sandburg in Chicago
John Sutter in Sacramento
Gloria Vanderbilt in New York
Edith Wilson in Washington

MOON OPPOSITE MC/CONJUNCT IC
- ideal place to establish the foundation you seek so desperately
- the feeling of belonging
- could remind you of your childhood home

- feelings run deep
- need for privacy and seclusion
- vivid imagination works overtime
- strong psychic hunches and intuition
- prone to change environment frequently
- loves to move around or redecorate
- professional issues often suffer
- should consider having an office in your home
- plays the role of a parent
- takes care of those less fortunate
- has conventional and traditional values
- great love for home and family

Al Capone in Chicago
Elizabeth I in London
F. S. Fitzgerald in Hollywood
U. S. Grant in Vicksburg
Bruce Jenner in Montreal
Helen Keller in New York
Wm. McKinley in Washington
Sir Thomas More in London
Muhammad Ali in Zaire
Napoleon I at Waterloo
Roman Polanski in Hollywood
Leontyne Price in New York
Gertrude Stein in Paris
Tchaikowsky in Leningrad
Boris Yeltsin in Moscow

MERCURY CONJUNCT ASC
- highly communicative and talkative
- willingly exchanges ideas
- fluent in speech but often fails to listen
- great wit and repartee
- high degree of intelligence
- good place for students, teachers or writers
- overly active mind is continually stimulated
- very eloquent with words
- periodic insomnia due to nervous conditions
- must learn to relax
- restless and changeable
- wants to be where the action is
- loves change for its own sake
- curious and inquisitive
- tendency to flit from one thing to the other
- hobbies often become profitable
- much attention to detail

Fatty Arbuckle in Hollywood
Catherine the Great in Leningrad
M. K. Gandhi in New Delhi
Giuseppe Garibaldi in Rome
Wm. Gladstone in London
Arthur Godfrey in Miami
J. Edgar Hoover in Washington
Groucho Marx in Hollywood
Edward R. Murrow in London
R. L. Stevenson in Samoa

MERCURY SEXTILE ASC
- life revolves around intellectual discussions
- others stimulate your mind
- involved with organizations which increase social life
- easy to make contacts
- many friends and acquaintances
- great need to keep busy
- free time is often spent looking for something productive to do
- energy burns up quickly just thinking about what to do next
- talent for writing and public speaking
- should develop more depth and sense of purpose
- often superficial and slapdash
- learn to complete one thing before beginning another
- good relations with neighbors and siblings
- good for any enterprise which requires being an entrepreneur

Roseanne Barr in Hollywood
Lenny Bruce in New York
Wm. J. Bryan in Washington
Richard Chamberlain in London
Chiang Kaishek in Taiwan
Walt Disney in Orlando
Adolph Eichmann in Berlin
W. G. Harding in San Francisco
Clark Gable in Hollywood
John XXIII in Rome
R. F. Kennedy in Los Angeles
Vivien Leigh in Hollywood
Douglas MacArthur in Tokyo
Michelangelo in Rome
Paderewski in Warsaw

George Patton in Frankfurt

MERCURY SQUARE ASC
- difficulty relating to others
- seldom gets their point across
- often misunderstood or misinterpreted statements cause worry or concern
- abundant nervous or mental energy
- too active for their own good
- often beats around the bush
- should stick to the central issue
- tendency to gossip or spread faulty information
- could make unfriendly remarks
- problems with speech, dialect or language
- could produce stuttering or dyslexia
- mind often races ahead of one's mouth
- highly critical and faultfinding
- often superficial or flighty
- poor judgment causes major crises

F. A. Bartholdi in New York
George Bush in Washington
Prince Charles in London
Walt Disney in Hollywood
R. W. Emerson in Boston
Francisco Franco in Madrid
Hindenburg in Berlin
Michael Jordan in Chicago
M. L. King in Atlanta
Jacqueline Onassis in Dallas
Nancy Reagan in Washington
Nelson Rockefeller in Washington
Albert Schweitzer in Gabon
Barbra Streisand in Hollywood

MERCURY TRINE ASC
- any outlets to stimulate your curious and overly active mind
- talents are recognized due to natural ability to express yourself with ease
- likes to be with people who are stimulating, interesting and exciting
- hobbies could become profitable
- all games and amusements favored
- ability to convince others through public speaking or journalism
- good for those attending colleges or universities

- good for all business concerns

Ray Bradbury in Hollywood
F. F. Coppola in Hollywood
Leonardo da Vinci in Florence
Mamie Eisenhower in Washington
Eugenie in Paris
John Fremont in San Francisco
Charles Gordon in the Sudan
Hirohito in Tokyo
Anver Joffrey in New York
Helen Keller in New York
Henry Kissinger in Washington
Alice R. Longworth in Washington
Wm. McKinley in Washington
Nelson Mandela in Cape Town
Josef Mengele in Auschwitz
Mary Pickford in Hollywood
Franz Schubert in Vienna
Tina Turner in Dallas
Vincent van Gogh in Arles
Giuseppe Verdi in Milan
Vanna White in Hollywood
William of Orange in London

MERCURY INCONJUNCT ASC
- problems with communication
- often says the exact opposite of what was meant
- speech difficulties surface such as stuttering or dyslexia
- few pay attention to what you say or grasp your meaning or intent
- others think you're opinionated when in fact they've already made up their minds about you
- highly analytical and critical
- very intense, sarcastic and vituperative in speech
- mental confusion clutters up one's ability to discriminate
- many mental compulsions and obsessions cause tunnel vision
- can't expand mental horizons
- nervousness could lead to insomnia or other mental disorders
- wants everything to be in its proper order or place

Beethoven in Vienna
E. B. Browning in Florence
Deng Xiaoping in Peking
Bob Fosse in New York
Bob Geldof in Ethiopia
Victor Hugo in Paris
Jim Jones in Guyana
J. F. Kennedy in Washington
Jack London in the Yukon
Imelda Marcos in Manila
Harvey Milk in San Francisco
Richard Nixon in Peking
F. D. Roosevelt in Campobello
Stanford White in New York

MERCURY OPP ASC/CONJUNCT DESC
- desires to communicate above all else
- passion often suffers in close relationships
- needs constant mental stimuli
- tries to compete intellectually
- often dominates the conversation
- loves to debate and argue
- generally high IQ fascinates others
- eloquent with words
- shies away from emotional intensity
- must be free to roam and explore
- works well with those who have the same level of intelligence
- favored for those in sales, public relations, the law or politics
- ability to influence the public
- fine voice and distinctive writing style

Gloria Allred in Los Angeles
Catherine of Aragon in London
Van Cliburn in Moscow
F. de Lesseps in Egypt
Cary Grant in Hollywood
Adolf Hitler in Berlin
Xaviera Hollander in New York
Nikolai Lenin in Leningrad
Joseph McCarthy in Washington
Robert Schumann in Leipzig
Steven Spielberg in Hollywood
F .L. Wright in Chicago

MERCURY CONJUNCT MC

- impresses others with one's intelligence
- good for communication on all levels
- writing ability and talent for public speaking
- good place to attend school or to do research
- has a passion for knowledge
- uses the mind to get ahead in life
- known for being witty and charming
- restlessness causes you to seek excitement and continual stimuli
- often a jack of all trades and a master of none
- many job changes
- bored easily
- good place to find work or to go into business
- always on the go
- need for constant variety
- makes many important social contacts
- studious and well read and informed about the latest issues

Jim Bakker in Charlotte
Yul Brynner in Hollywood
George Bush in Washington
R. W. Emerson in Boston
Greta Garbo in Hollywood
John XXIII in Rome
Jack London in the Yukon
Josef Mengele in Auschwitz
Nicholas II in Leningrad
Jacqueline Onassis in Dallas
Mme de Pompadour in Paris
Dan Quayle in Washington
Nancy Reagan in Washington
Eleanor Roosevelt in Washington
Babe Ruth in New York
Franz Schubert in Vienna
Rod Serling in Hollywood
Elizabeth Taylor in Hollywood
George Washington in Philadelphia
Boris Yeltsin in Moscow

MERCURY SEXTILE MC

- plans for the future with intelligence
- develops skills needed for future survival
- places priorities in proper order
- chooses one's words wisely

- those in superior positions recognize your viewpoint and accept your ideas
- domestic and professional life is well balanced
- serious about the future
- relates well to young people and those who seek to learn and explore
- desire for public speaking or writing
- ability to influence others
- many social engagements which advances the career
- strong investigative ability likes to get to the bottom of things

Catherine of Aragon in London
John Barrymore in Hollywood
Melvin Belli in San Francisco
Lizzie Borden in Fall River
Rosalynn Carter in Washington
Cher in Hollywood
Calvin Coolidge in Washington
Walter Cronkhite in New York
Henry Ford II in Detroit
Reinhard Heydrich in Berlin
J. F. Kennedy in Washington
D. H. Lawrence in Taos
David Lloyd George in London
Imelda Marcos in Manila
Aimee S. McPherson in Los Angeles
Bette Midler in Hollywood
Sydney Omarr in Hollywood
Gavrilo Princip in Sarajevo
Knute Rockne in South Bend
Father Serra in California
John Steinbeck in Salinas
Patrick Swayze in Hollywood
Voltaire in Paris

MERCURY SQUARE MC

- obstacles placed in the path of effective communication
- difficult to separate what one thinks from what one feels
- often loses sight of the central issue
- highly emotional delivery
- mind works overtime
- needs continual mental variety and stimuli
- wavers from one idea to another

- often gets bored and drops the matter
- fails to recognize what others are telling you
- must learn to listen
- big mouth lands you in hot water
- has "foot in mouth" disease
- problems with speech or language
- very changeable and indecisive
- has many weird or eccentric notions
- often overestimates one's ability
- often aimless and vacillating
- failure comes from lack of motivation

Fatty Arbuckle in Hollywood
Helena Blavatsky in New York
Marlon Brando in Tahiti
Catherine de Medici in Paris
Alexandre Dumas in Paris
Arthur Godfrey in Miami
Bruno Hauptmann in New York
Janis Joplin in San Francisco
Nikolai Lenin in Zurich
Abraham Lincoln in Washington
Louis XVI in Paris
Groucho Marx in Hollywood
Yoko Ono in New York
Lowell Thomas in Lhasa
Jack Valenti in Hollywood

MERCURY TRINE MC

- willing to study methods necessary to further career
- conventional views sit well with those in superior positions
- communication comes easily
- enjoys playing games and reading
- ability to influence others
- good for public speaking or writing
- relates well to children on their level
- loves to tell stories
- home should have a large library or den
- hobbies may turn profitable
- good for all business ventures
- often known as an intellectual lion
- abundant talents don't go unnoticed
- need for variety furthers ambition
- loves to travel and explore

Ann Margret in Hollywood
Brigitte Bardot in Paris
Marlon Brando in Hollywood
E. B. Browning in Florence
Carol Burnett in Hollywood
Neville Chamberlain in Munich
Richard Chamberlain in London
Thomas Edison in Menlo Park
D. D. Eisenhower in Washington
Errol Flynn in Hollywood
Dag Hammarksjold in New York
Ted Kennedy in Washington
Nikolai Lenin in Moscow
Sir Thomas More in London
Mozart in Vienna
Manuel Noriega in Panama City
Elvis Presley in Memphis
Cecil Rhodes in Rhodesia
F. D. Roosevelt in Campobello
Grace Slick in San Francisco
Mark Spitz in Munich
Arturo Toscanini in New York
Pierre Trudeau in Ottawa
Mark Twain in San Francisco
Giuseppe Verdi in Milan
William of Orange in London

MERCURY INCONJUNCT MC

- conflict between what one thinks they want from life and how they feel about matters after getting it
- overly analytical with strong critical faculties
- many opportunities for advancement are missed due to bad timing
- dichotomy between what one says and does
- contradictory and perverse
- mentally indecisive and continually sits on the fence
- worries about the little things and fails to see the big picture
- often goes with the line of least resistance
- could be dishonest, a liar, cheat or thief

Martin Bormann in Berlin
Christian Dior in Paris
Walt Disney in Orlando
Jane Fonda in Hanoi

John Fremont in San Francisco
Vivien Leigh in Hollywood
Liberace in Las Vegas
Alice R. Longworth in Washington
Machiavelli in Florence
Oliver North in Washington
Louis Pasteur in Paris
George Patton in Frankfurt
Duke of Wellington at Waterloo

MERCURY OPP MC/CONJUNCT IC
- great interest in historical matters
- researches the family tree
- well developed psychic and intuitive abilities
- penchant for investigation or psychology
- likes to get to the bottom of things
- often gets so wrapped up in one's thoughts that
  the outside world passes unnoticed
- loves to travel and explore
- should live in a mobile home
- strongly patriotic and nationalistic
- relates well to young people
- conventional and family oriented
- many changes of residence
- loves to redecorate or enlarge the home

Walt Disney in Hollywood
Francisco Franco in Madrid
Joseph Goebbels in Berlin
Ferdinand Marcos in Manila
Muhammad Ali in Zaire
Bishop Pike in Israel
George Sand in Paris
Norman Schwarzkopf in Kuwait
Albert Schweitzer in Gabon

VENUS CONJUNCT ASC
- pleasant and comfortable environment
- appearances count a lot
- very vain
- one of the best places for love and romance
- relationships prosper
- appealing and attractive to others
- great charm and magnetism
- strong appreciation of beauty
- often involved in the cultural scene
- very conscious of social status

- sometimes a snob or social climber
- often lazy and passive in relationships
- could fall victim to those with stronger personalities
- sometimes self-indulgent
- sexual promiscuity or weight gain should be curbed
- highly acquisitive
- possessive of people and things
- jealousy and envy often prominent
- conscious of good taste or manners
- usually well-bred and gracious

Michael Bennett in New York
Jane Fonda in Hollywood
Gerald Ford in Washington
Judy Garland in New York
Arthur Godfrey in Miami
Helmut Kohl in Bonn
Michael Landon in Hollywood
Paderewski in Warsaw

VENUS SEXTILE ASC
- many opportunities for social contacts
- cheerful and diplomatic disposition
- can be counted on to do the right thing at the right time
- associates with artistic or cultural types
- makes friends easily
- very popular on the party circuit
- conscious of propriety and etiquette
- even tempered and warm hearted
- often a dilettante or superficial butterfly
- very concerned with appearances
- wants to be admired
- susceptible to flattery
- overly gullible at times

Ansel Adams in Yosemite
Lizzie Borden in Fall River
Eva Braun in Berlin
Barbara Cartland in London
Edward VII in London
M. K. Gandhi in Johannesburg
Christopher Isherwood in Berlin
John XXIII in Rome
M. L. King in Atlanta

Marie of Romania in Bucharest
Lord Mountbatten in New Delhi
William McKinley in Washington
Nicholas II in Leningrad
Paul Vi in Rome
Eva Peron in Buenos Aires
Juan Peron in Buenos Aires
Edith Piaf in Paris
Mark Spitz in Munich
Brigham Young in Salt Lake City

VENUS SQUARE ASC
- difficulty projecting oneself in a socially acceptable manner
- relationships fraught with tension and stress
- often shuns the social scene altogether
- likes weird, odd or funky types
- overly sensitive to opinions of others
- takes offense at the slightest inference
- sincerity questionable
- could flatter to get the upper hand
- can be hypocritical
- sometimes lazy and vain
- doesn't pull their own weight most of the time
- often indifferent to the needs of others
- little patience with long term liaisons
- sexual promiscuity an outlet for loneliness
- pleasure seeking and self indulgent
- sometimes pretentious
- often wastes one's talents

Pearl Buck in Nanking
Andrew Carnegie in Pittsburgh
Ray Bradbury in Hollywood
Fidel Castro in Havana
F .F. Coppola in Hollywood
Eugenie in Paris
Harrison Ford in Hollywood
Alfred Hitchcock in Hollywood
Henry Kissinger in Washington
Peter Max in New York
Muhammad Ali in Zaire
Nehru in New Delhi
Florence Nightingale in the Crimea
George Patton in Frankfurt
Ronald Reagan in Hollywood
Nelson Rockefeller in Washington

Anwar Sadat in Cairo
P. B. Shelley in Italy
Gloria Steinem in New York
Wm. H. Taft in Washington
Tokyo Rose in Tokyo
Joseph Wambaugh in Los Angeles

VENUS TRINE ASC
- pleasing and agreeable personality in great demand with the social set
- great popularity
- strong artistic or cultural interests
- likes to surround oneself with beauty
- highly aesthetic
- often falls in love with love
- likes to be involved with romance all the time
- often lazy and self indulgent
- would rather play than work
- appreciates for one's appearance, manners, sense of style , decorum and sense of propriety
- latent artistic or musical talent should be exploited
- purchases items for their intrinsic value
- appreciates quality rather than quantity

Josephine Baker in Paris
Chiang Kaishek in Taiwan
Walt Disney in Orlando
Phil Donahue in New York
Henry Ford II in Detroit
Haydn in Vienna
Rudolf Hess in Berlin
James Huberty in San Diego
Stacy Keach in London
J. F. Kennedy in Washington
Jack Kerouac in San Francisco
Nikolai Lenin in Moscow
John Lennon in New York
Mata Hari in Paris
Michelangelo in Rome
Bette Midler in New York
Benito Mussolini in Rome
Jacqueline Onassis in Greece
Lee H. Oswald in Dallas
Wm. Rehnquist in Washington
Tom Selleck in Honolulu
Adlai Stevenson in New York

VENUS INCONJUNCT ASC
- difficulty relating to others due to extreme shyness or timidity
- reserved nature seldom invites intimacy
- needs much privacy and seclusion
- views relationships from a material standpoint
- great need for social acceptance
- very vulnerable and gullible
- questions one's virility or performance
- critical and intense with others
- often forced to surrender or sacrifice one's own desires
- wants to serve
- lacks self confidence
- asks few favors from others

Queen Anne in London
Rosa Bonheur in Paris
Barbara Bush in Washington
Van Cliburn in Moscow
Ava Gardner in Hollywood
F. de Lesseps in Suez
Walt Disney in Hollywood
Indira Gandhi in New Delhi
Christine Jorgensen in Denmark
Helen Keller in New York
Mary Pickford in Hollywood
Bishop Pike in Israel
Dan Rather in New York
Robert Redford in Utah
Henry Thoreau in Concord
Duke of Wellington at Waterloo
Kaiser Wilhelm II in Berlin
Boris Yeltsin in Moscow

VENUS OPP ASC/CONJUNCT DESC
- harmonious married life with many pleasant memories
- adept when dealing with others
- always gracious and tactful
- very popular with the social set
- a team player who goes along with the crowd
- prefers intimate liaisons
- hates the singles scene or one night stands
- seeks approval from others
- needs much love and affection
- others usually call the shots
- must learn to be more independent
- takes pride in appearance
- wants an artistic or cultured partner
- makes few real enemies
- tries to avoid conflict
- will settle for peace at any price
- laziness often attracts those who use you for their own selfish gain

Pablo Casals in San Juan
Frederic Chopin in Paris
Joan Crawford in Hollywood
Bob Geldof in Ethiopia
Reinhard Heydrich in Berlin
Alice R. Longworth in Washington
Nelson Mandela in Johannesburg
Harvey Milk in San Francisco
Rupert Murdoch in London
Gavrilo Princip in Sarajevo
Theodore Roosevelt in Washington
Elizabeth Taylor in Rome

VENUS CONJUNCT MC
- work involving the arts, culture, music, public relations or diplomacy favored
- charms one's way into the boardroom
- socially ambitious and status conscious
- pleasing appearance, fine manners, elegance and a sense of style wins many points in your favor
- status often improves through marriage
- could wed the boss' son or daughter
- money is important
- must learn to budget due to overspending
- tries to keep up with the Joneses
- instinctively knows what the public wants
- often lazy or self indulgent
- love and affection generously given and warmly received
- often concentrates on surface appearances
- could become a shallow peacock
- contacts with women become important and profitable
- always loving and generous

Beethoven in Vienna
Otto von Bismarck in Berlin
Pearl Buck in Nanking

Mamie Eisenhower in Washington
Harrison Ford in Hollywood
Henry VIII in London
Rudolf Hess in Berlin
John XXIII in Rome
Grace Kelly in Monaco
R. F. Kennedy in Washington
Marie of Romania in Bucharest
A. S. McPherson in Los Angeles
J. K. Polk in Washington
Mme de Pompadour in Paris
Nelson Rockefeller in Washington
Erwin Rommel in El Alamein
Babe Ruth in New York

VENUS SEXTILE MC

- willing to make compromises necessary for success and happiness
- socially oriented
- hates conflict
- tries to create peace and harmony
- seeks approval from those in power and authority
- needs to be accepted
- receives support from family members
- kind, gentle and affectionate
- wants beauty and simplicity in the environment
- should work in a garden
- all real estate matters favored
- home could appreciate considerably over the years
- pleasant and agreeable love life
- many opportunities for romance

Marlon Brando in Tahiti
Al Capone in Chicago
Benjamin Disraeli in London
Adolph Eichmann in Berlin
D. D. Eisenhower in Washington
U. S. Grant in Vicksburg
Nikita Khrushchev in Moscow
Shirley MacLaine in Hollywood
Pat Nixon in Washington
Jacqueline Onassis in Washington
John Steinbeck in Salinas
Barbara Walters in New York
Earl Warren in Washington

George Washington in Philadelphia

VENUS SQUARE MC

- love and affection assume overwhelming importance
- works hard to insure that romance succeeds
- will lie or flatter if necessary
- honesty and sincerity are questionable
- often compromises one's own standards
- attracts lazy people who use you to further their own ambition
- problems with jealousy or possessiveness
- office love affairs are verboten
- little patience dealing with others on a daily basis
- should try to live alone
- could be considered a womanizer or gold digger
- will marry for status or money
- vain and egocentric
- often self indulgent or dissipated
- pleasure oriented and highly conceited
- many problems with women
- superficial in relationships
- difficulty in making commitments

Gloria Allred in Los Angeles
Marlon Brando in Hollywood
Enrico Caruso in New York
Rajiv Gandhi in New Delhi
George VI in London
Mel Gibson in Sydney
Arthur Godfrey in Miami
Bruno Hauptmann in New York
William Holden in Hollywood
Ethel Kennedy in Washington
Liberace in Las Vegas
Alice R. Longworth in Washington
Madonna in Hollywood
Leontyne Price in New York
Tchaikowsky in Leningrad
Margaret Thatcher in London
Ted Turner in Hollywood
Andy Warhol in New York
Kaiser Wilhelm II in Berlin

VENUS TRINE MC

- ability to charm others

- much grace, tact and diplomacy
- often lets others take the lead
- hates to be left alone
- highly acquisitive
- likes to surround oneself with objects of beauty or value
- pleasant domestic scene
- likes to party
- needs approval from outsiders
- relations with those in power are non-threatening
- highly cooperative, a real team player
- works well with clubs or organizations
- manages money wisely
- marriage usually succeeds but many opportunities for romance are always present
- multiple artistic and creative talents
- strong appreciation for music

Helen Gurley Brown in New York
Leonardo da Vinci in Florence
Henry Ford in Detroit
Indira Gandhi in New Delhi
James Hoffa in Detroit
Douglas MacArthur in Tokyo
Catherine de Medici in Paris
Robert Redford in Utah
Carroll Righter in Hollywood
George Sand in Paris
Robert Schumann in Leipzig
Richard Wagner in Bayreuth

VENUS INCONJUNCT MC
- an overwhelming need to be loved and appreciated
- obsessed with creating the right impression
- often considers oneself unworthy
- little faith in one's ability to love
- sometimes a liar or pretentious
- often sends out the wrong signals
- could rely on false impressions
- makes sacrifices in love
- often gives up the search for love altogether
- compulsive need for romance and sex
- hates to be left alone
- should live alone however
- lack of understanding about the true nature of love

- many misunderstandings or misconceptions
- often unwilling to accept the love that others do offer

Carol Burnett in Hollywood
B. Cellini in Florence
Walt Disney in Orlando
Jane Fonda in Hanoi
Judy Garland in Hollywood
Howard Hughes in Las Vegas
Jim Jones in Guyana
Abraham Lincoln in Washington
Pablo Picasso in Paris
Bhagwan Rajneesh in Oregon
Diana Spencer in London
Leopold Stokowski in New York
Shirley Temple in Hollywood
Mark Twain in San Francisco
Duke of Wellington in Waterloo
Frank Lloyd Wright in Chicago

VENUS OPPOSITE MC/CONJUNCT IC
- peaceful and harmonious domestic life filled with comfort, luxury and ease
- wants peace and quiet
- needs a place to relax and unwind
- strives for security and stability
- interest in history and genealogy
- home filled with many objects of beauty of great value
- money is spent lavishly on one's surroundings
- loves to redecorate the home
- love of tradition or patriotism
- rather conventional and family oriented
- parental relations are peaceful
- much affection given and received from family members
- women exert a strong influence on one's outlook

Andrew Carnegie in Pittsburgh
Prince Charles in London
Marion Davies in Hollywood
Christopher Isherwood in Berlin
Margaret Mead in Samoa
George Patton in Frankfurt
Anwar Sadat in Cairo
R. L. Stevenson in Samoa

MARS CONJUNCT ASC

- reputation for being intense, domineering or courageous
- life is often a battle for survival
- possibility of injuries or accidents
- extremely aggressive and always assertive
- a strong undercurrent of violence
- passionate and jealous
- sometimes cruel or selfish
- a real fighter
- great deal of physical energy
- good for those involved in sports
- the chase is more important than the catch in romantic matters
- highly sexual
- attacks life with gusto
- fearless, impatient, brash and daring
- prefers to do things alone
- find it difficult to cooperate
- hates to wait for anything or anyone
- often imposes one's will on others
- possible contacts with the military or the police
- good environment for soldiers

Lord Byron in Greece
Truman Capote in New York
Rosalynn Carter in Washington
Mary Cassatt in Paris
John DeLorean in Detroit
Christian Dior in Paris
Arthur Conan Doyle in London
Betty Ford in Washington
Antonio Gaudi in Barcelona
William Holden in Hollywood
Johann Strauss in Vienna

- hates people who make demands on one's time or energy
- agitated if forced to remain in one place for very long
- fond of sports
- many opportunities for sexual liaisons

F. A. Bartholdi in New York
Marlon Brando in Hollywood
Wm. J. Bryan in Washington
Calvin Coolidge in Washington
M. K. Gandhi in Johannesburg
Giuseppe Garibaldi in Rome
Jean Genet in Paris
Katharine Hepburn in Hollywood
Rock Hudson in Hollywood
Bruce Jenner in Montreal
Grace Kelly in Hollywood
Lafayette in Philadelphia
Timothy Leary in San Francisco
Margaret Mead in Samoa
Francois Mitterand in Paris
Napoleon I in Moscow
Florence Nightingale in the Crimea
Aristotle Onassis in Buenos Aires
Jacqueline Onassis in Washington
William Penn in Philadelphia
Pius XII in Rome
Elvis Presley in Memphis
Bhagwan Rajneesh in Oregon
Wm. Rehnquist in Washington
R. L. Stevenson in Samoa
Harry Truman in Hiroshima
Mark Twain in San Francisco
Duke of Windsor in London

MARS SEXTILE ASC

- a natural leader
- enthusiasm causes others to follow
- creates interest in group participation
- asserts oneself with ease
- forceful, frank and direct
- wastes little time on the niceties
- honest and candid
- fights for truth or personal beliefs
- likes those who are independent and active
- very decisive and stubborn

MARS SQUARE ASC

- forces one's personality on others
- violence often surrounds the individual
- prefers to do things alone
- almost impossible to really cooperate harmoniously
- fights and disputes arise due to hair-trigger temper
- frustration and anger erupt when you can't be number one

- projects an aggressive manner like a street fighter or bully
- impetuous and impatient
- quarrelsome and contentious
- often abusive and coarse
- needs to learn social graces and etiquette
- walks around with a chip on one's shoulder
- highly sexed
- loves the conquest and forces others to submit or surrender

Ann Margret in Hollywood
Michael Bennett in New York
Richard Burton in Hollywood
Mother Cabrini in New York
Catherine de Medici in Paris
Richard Chamberlain in London
Captain Cook in Sydney
Father Damien in Hawaii
Jesse Helms in Washington
Groucho Marx in Hollywood
Manuel Noriega in Panama
Louis Pasteur in Paris
Leontyne Price in New York
Nancy Reagan in Washington
F.D. Roosevelt on Campobello
Leon Trotsky in Leningrad
Andy Warhol in New York

MARS TRINE ASC
- strong-willed, courageous and daring
- capacity for leadership
- highly independent
- craves freedom of movement and thought
- works well with others
- enters projects wholeheartedly and with vigor
- great physical endurance and vitality
- shuns others with less strength or will power
- enjoys sporting events
- many opportunities for sexual liaisons
- exuberant and enthusiastic outlook on life which is infectious to others
- strong ideals and beliefs
- a crusader who fights to the bitter end
- decisive and persistent
- determined to succeed
- needs always to be active

Brigitte Bardot in Paris
Melvin Belli in San Francisco
Captain Bligh in Tahiti
Lizzie Borden in Fall River
King Charles I in London
Bobby Fischer in Iceland
Hirohito in Tokyo
J. Edgar Hoover in Washington
Aldous Huxley in Hollywood
Abraham Lincoln in Washington
J.K. Polk in Washington
Gavrilo Princip ion Sarajevo
Albert Speer in Berlin
Robert Urich in Boston

MARS INCONJUNCT ASC
- dilemma between cooperation or remaining dependent on others
- uncompromising manner makes it difficult to relate well
- expresses oneself in a more aggressive manner than is called for
- often can't back up one's threats or boasts
- exaggerates one's accomplishments
- impatient but often burns one's bridges behind them
- irritated and frustrated by things one cannot control or dominate
- often intimidates strangers
- sex is often used as a weapon
- others are often repulsed by your forceful manner
- should cultivate social grace

Jane Addams in Chicago
E. B. Browning in Florence
Eva Braun in Berlin
Judy Garland in New York
Cary Grant in Hollywood
Rudolf Hess in Berlin
J. F. Kennedy in Washington
Richard Nixon in Peking
Ronald Reagan in Hollywood
Oral Roberts in Tulsa
Steven Spielberg in Hollywood
Leopold Stokowski in New York
Toulouse Lautrec in Paris

Jack Valenti in Hollywood
Gloria Vanderbilt in New York

MARS OPPOSITE ASC/CONJ DESC
- prefers to take the initiative
- hard to let others take the lead
- problems arise with cooperation
- always passionate or combative
- often acts defensively
- highly sensitive to criticism or direction
- strong willed and aggressive
- loves to dispute, argue or fight
- provokes violence or antipathy
- reacts in a hostile or threatening manner
- must have complete freedom and independence
- won't be tied down by anyone
- respects people who give you space to do your own thing
- not very good for marital harmony

Coco Chanel in Paris
John Dillinger in Chicago
Haydn in Vienna
Heinrich Himmler in Berlin
Howard Hughes in Las Vegas
John XXIII in Rome
Jim Jones in Guyana
Douglas MacArthur in Tokyo
Charles Manson in Los Angeles
Carl Sandburg in Chicago
Henry Thoreau in Concord
George Washington in Philadelphia

MARS CONJUNCT MC
- reputation as a workaholic
- strives for success
- great deal of concentration
- never afraid to take the initiative
- hates to take orders from anyone
- great ambition for power and control
- assumes the role of an authority
- highly competitive nature wears down adversaries
- very macho outlook on life
- organized and persistent
- great physical energy and endurance
- military demeanor like a staff sergeant

- could become a dictator or tyrant
- headstrong and self-centered
- works best when working alone
- often coarse and unrefined
- needs freedom to explore
- often known as a pioneer
- highly sexual aura demands complete submission
- considerable ambition and drive
- purposeful and pragmatic
- little time for fantasy as reality always wins in the end

Captain Cook in Sydney
Zsa Zsa Gabor in Hollywood
Ava Gardner in Hollywood
Jean Genet in Paris
Whoopi Goldberg in Hollywood
W. G. Harding in San Francisco
Nancy Reagan in Washington
F. D. Roosevelt on Campobello
Shah of Iran in Teheran
Wm. H. Taft in Washington
Andy Warhol in New York

MARS SEXTILE MC
- personal and professional matters succeed providing one takes the initiative
- works well alone or in groups
- takes life seriously
- self sufficient and self confident
- wastes little time on the frills
- determined and purposeful
- wants immediate results
- authority figures teach you self reliance and independence
- organized and resolute
- ambitious and resourceful
- very businesslike manner
- appears like an authority on most issues
- highly constructive
- good for soldiers, engineers or surgeons

Josephine Baker in Paris
Wm. J. Bryan in Washington
Catherine of Aragon in London
Chiang Kaishek in Taiwan

F. de Lesseps in Suez
Tom Dooley in Laos
Adolph Eichmann in Jerusalem
Jerry Falwell in Lynchburg
Judy Garland in Hollywood
Harrison Ford in Hollywood
Lee Iacocca in Detroit
Juan Carlos in Madrid
J. F. Kennedy in Washington
Krishnamurti in Ojai
Charles Lindbergh in Paris
H. Ross Perot in Dallas
Joseph Smith in Nauvoo
Tina Turner in Dallas
F. L. Wright in Chicago

MARS SQUARE MC
- difficulty dealing with authority figures
- wants to be number one
- professional and domestic life fraught with tension and stress
- impulsive nature could make for confrontation with the police or military
- resents anyone who tries to manage or direct you
- often one's own worst enemy
- refuses to heed advice or counsel
- short sighted nature leads to ruin
- relies on momentary gratification
- suspicious of those who try to change you
- highly aggressive and impulsive
- loves to pick a fight
- strong inferiority complex
- hides sensitivity behind a mask of anger or hostility
- needs to prove oneself sexually
- requires surrender or submission

Konrad Adenauer in Bonn
Carol Burnett in Hollywood
George Bush in Washington
Henry Ford in Detroit
Haydn in Vienna
William Gladstone in London
Hugh Hefner in Hollywood
William Holden in Hollywood
Howard Hughes in Las Vegas
Joseph McCarthy in Washington

Marcel Proust in Paris
James Earl Ray in Memphis
Carl Sandburg in Chicago
P. B. Shelley in Italy
Tiberius in Rome

MARS TRINE MC
- determined and persistent
- energetic and hard working
- great success possible
- has respect of those in power and authority
- few illusions about one's purpose or personality
- abundant physical energy
- little need to control or dominate others
- even tempered and seldom petulant
- wastes little time on displays of anger
- works fast and furiously
- well organized and efficient
- independent but not very competitive
- prefers to work alone
- prefers to be responsible for one's own decisions and failures
- many romantic encounters
- loves sex, especially the chase

E. B. Browning in Florence
Coco Chanel in Paris
Mme du Barry in Paris
Bob Fosse in New York
Indira Gandhi in New Delhi
Henry VIII in London
Heinrich Himmler in Berlin
Ted Kennedy in Washington
Machiavelli in Florence
Bernard Montgomery in El Alamein
J. P. Morgan in New York
Edward R. Murrow in London
Robespierre in Paris
Albert Speer in Berlin
Jack Valenti in Hollywood
Duke of Windsor in London

MARS INCONJUNCT MC
- mixed feelings about those in power and authority including the parents
- needs guidance and direction but finds it hard to take orders from anyone

- often bends the rules in order to succeed or be noticed
- continual tug of war between self assertion and the need for compromise
- strong destructive nature
- highly intense and obsessive
- confrontations with the police or military
- often a criminal or petty lawbreaker
- hardship and frustration concerning possessions
- always seems to want more than one can afford
- wants to be number one or nothing at all
- won't settle for second best

Gloria Allred in Los Angeles
Beethoven in Vienna
Lizzie Borden in Fall River
Cellini in Florence
Richard Chamberlain in London
Van Cliburn in Moscow
Bobby Fischer in Iceland
Diane von Furstenburg in New York
U. S. Grant in Vicksburg
Leona Helmsley in New York
Rock Hudson in Hollywood
Grace Kelly in Hollywood
M. L. King in Memphis
Henry Kissinger in Washington
Billy Martin in New York
Maximilian in Mexico
Michelangelo in Rome
Francois Mitterand in Paris
Robert Redford in Utah
Norman Schwarzkopf in Kuwait
R. L. Stevenson in Samoa
Barbra Streisand in Hollywood
Robert Urich in Boston
Stanford White in New York
Yogananda in Los Angeles

MARS OPPOSITE MC/CONJ IC
- confrontations and lack of harmony on the home front
- forceful and combative nature challenges parental authority
- compulsive and rash
- many accidents in the home
- needs space to roam and explore

- loves to "rough it" every now and then
- spartan, austere and rigorous domestic life
- likes to rule the roost with an iron hand
- often refuses to compromise
- good repairman around the house
- loves to reconstruct what has gone wrong
- insecurity about one's sexual role
- continually needs to prove oneself

Johannes Brahms in Vienna
Fidel Castro in Havana
Father Damien in Hawaii
Che Guevara in Havana
Christine Jorgensen in Denmark
Groucho Marx in Hollywood
Harvey Milk in San Francisco
Rupert Murdoch in New York

JUPITER CONJUNCT ASC
- considerable good luck, success and prosperity
- optimistic, positive and extrovertive manner wins points in your favor
- much faith in the goodness of mankind
- benevolent and magnanimous
- sometimes self righteous, pompous, pretentious or snobby
- wants the very best and won't settle for anything second rate
- strong missionary spirit infects others with your enthusiasm
- expresses oneself in a grandiose and dramatic way
- tries to live life in the grand manner
- tries to be ethical, moral and upright
- tolerant and understanding of others' idiosyncrasies and eccentricities
- likes to keep things pure and simple
- expects freedom and independence
- interested in religion and philosophy
- loves to travel and explore
- often extravagant
- tendency to gain weight
- fondness for luxury and ease

Irving Berlin in New York
Helena Blavatsky in New York
Father Damien in Hawaii

Deng Xiaoping in Peking
Benjamin Disraeli in London
Mme du Barry in Paris
Edward VII in London
R. W. Emerson in Boston
Rajiv Gandhi in New Delhi
U. S. Grant in Vicksburg
Ernest Hemingway in Paris
L. B. Johnson in Washington
M. L. King in Memphis
Maria Theresa in Vienna
Napoleon I in Cairo
Theodore Roosevelt in Washington
Artur Rubinstein in New york
Babe Ruth in New York
Albert Schweitzer in Gabon
Johann Strauss in Vienna
John Sutter in Sacramento
Brigham Young in Salt Lake City

Alice R. Longworth in Washington
Martin Luther in Wittenberg
Margaret Mead in Samoa
Manuel Noriega in Panama
Rudolph Nureyev in New York
Dan Rather in New York
Nelson Rockefeller in Washington
Tom Selleck in Honolulu
Margaret Thatcher in London
Voltaire in Paris
Duke of Wellington at Waterloo

JUPITER SEXTILE ASC

- popularity gains support and cooperation from those in power and authority
- generous and optimistic to a fault
- idealistic and romantic
- enthusiasm causes others to follow your lead
- partnerships and marriage successful
- a nice person to have around
- little trouble making or keeping friends
- prefers to associate with the wealthy
- always wants to help others
- tries to make a good impression
- quick to take advantage of an opportunity
- ability to charm
- expresses oneself in a grandiose, dramatic and regal manner
- interested in social improvement
- strong religious bent

JUPITER SQUARE ASC

- demands a lot from oneself and from others
- often extravagant or bossy
- often goes overboard or to excess
- wants the biggest or the most costly
- often bombastic, pompous or self righteous
- does things in the grand manner
- sometimes spreads oneself too thin
- wants to be where the action is
- budgets are often strained
- credit problems and possible bankruptcy
- tries to impress others with one's wealth, success or influence
- often hypocritical or conceited
- often wastes talents or abilities
- desires to be a person of importance

Andrew Carnegie in Pittsburgh
Marie Curie in Paris
James Dean in Hollywood
Anne Frank in Amsterdam
Jean Harlow in Hollywood
Heinrich Himmler in Berlin
L. Ron Hubbard in Los Angeles
Victor Hugo in Paris

Barbara Cartland in London
Van Cliburn in Moscow
Errol Flynn in Hollywood
Howard Hughes in Las Vegas
Bruce Jenner in Montreal
Christine Jorgensen in Denmark
Carl Jung in Zurich
G. Gordon Liddy in Washington
Bernard Montgomery in El Alamein
Lee H. Oswald in Dallas
Mary Pickford in Hollywood
Mme de Pompadour in Paris
J. D. Rockefeller in Cleveland
Anwar Sadat in Cairo
Carl Sandburg in Chicago
Father Serra in San Diego
Mark Twain in San Francisco
Edith Wilson in Washington

Yogananda in Los Angeles

JUPITER TRINE ASC
- conservative and optimistic attitude
- broad outlook on life
- abundant self confidence inspires good will and enthusiasm
- positive approach
- happiness in personal, professional or domestic levels
- good sense of humor
- loves the social whirl and party circuit
- charms one's way in or out of any situation
- popular and tolerant
- desires to experience as much as possible
- wants freedom to roam and explore
- good for students or scholars
- curious about foreign cultures or languages
- upright, moral and ethical
- religious or legal matters favored
- good storyteller makes one the center of attention
- well respected and recognized for one's talents

Ingrid Bergman in Rome
Edgar Cayce in Virginia Beach
Frederic Chopin in Paris
Joan Collins in Hollywood
Charles Darwin in the Galapagos
Mary Baker Eddy in Boston
M. K. Gandhi in Johannesburg
Judy Garland in Hollywood
Whoopi Goldberg in Hollywood
Gary Hart in Miami
Lady Bird Johnson in Washington
Groucho Marx in Hollywood
Edith Piaf in Paris
James Earl Ray in Memphis
Ronald Reagan in Washington
Robert Redford in Utah
George Sand in Paris
Arturo Toscanini in New York
Oscar Wilde in Paris
Woodrow Wilson in Paris

JUPITER INCONJUNCT ASC
- environment changes radically from one day to the next
- tries to be helpful to those who are down and out
- sometimes tries to evade responsibility
- wants freedom but things crop up which change basic plans
- often called upon to play the role of savior
- others think you have all the answers
- grand visions and aspirations
- often has no funds to foot the bill
- prefers to live in the grand manner
- hates to worry or fret

Gloria Allred in Los Angeles
Warren Beatty in Hollywood
Captain Bligh in Tahiti
Charles Chaplin in Hollywood
Francisco Goya in Madrid
Liberace in Las Vegas
James Madison in Washington
Audie Murphy in France
Sydney Omarr in Hollywood
Yoko Ono in New York
Pius XII in Rome
Tchaikowsky in Leningrad
Gloria Vanderbilt in New York

JUPITER OPPOSITE ASC/CONJ DESC
- good fortune through close, intimate relationships or marriage
- public contacts fortunate
- instinctive knowledge of public needs
- others respond to you in a positive manner
- basic interest in their welfare
- sometimes hypocritical just to serve your own selfish ambitions
- wants to be with those who help you to grow
- seeks to expand basic consciousness
- likes those from foreign cultures, different ethnic groups or religions
- restlessness makes it hard to settle down
- always seeking greener pastures
- freedom is one's most prized possession
- won't let others tie you down
- support and assistance comes easily

- all favors returned generously
- some see you as an all knowing "guru" and expect you to guide them

Ann Margret in Hollywood
Pearl Buck in Nanking
Catherine de Medici in Paris
Hindenburg in Berlin
J. Edgar Hoover in Washington
Janis Joplin in San Francisco
Lafayette in Philadelphia
Frank Sinatra in Hollywood
John Steinbeck in Salinas
Wm. H. Taft in Washington

JUPITER CONJUNCT MC
- success comes from making important and influential social contacts
- rich and powerful people are drawn to you
- much esteem and recognition
- life is easy and fame comes with little effort
- possibility of great wealth
- always honest and direct
- receives support and admiration from those who count
- fighter for truth and justice
- religious and legal matters go well
- very high standards and ideals
- won't compromise one's integrity or honor
- popularity and publicity
- life lived in the limelight
- good for politicians or actors
- has the ability to influence the public
- often self indulgent
- lives beyond one's means
- must learn to budget and save
- noble and optimistic outlook
- very expansive and generally lucky

Helena Blavatsky in London
Truman Capote in New York
Chiang Kaishek in Taiwan
John DeLorean in Detroit
D. D. Eisenhower in Washington
Betty Ford in Washington
George VI in London
W. G. Harding in Washington

Heinrich Himmler in Berlin
William Holden in Hollywood
Howard Hughes in Las Vegas
Rudyard Kipling in London
Marie of Romania in Bucharest
Auguste Rodin in Paris
Anwar Sadat in Cairo
Harry Truman in Washington
Duke of Wellington at Waterloo

JUPITER SEXTILE MC
- professional success and good fortune due to strong sense of purpose
- good reputation among friends, associates and those in superior positions
- many opportunities to expand horizons and basic understanding
- eclectic outlook on life
- avid student or researcher
- ability to make others work for a common cause
- gains support as well as money
- authority figures recognize maturity and stability
- highly conventional and traditional
- restlessness causes you to want to be in two places at the same time
- much overall happiness and comfort
- civilized and humane attitude towards others

Captain Bligh in Tahiti
C. B. deMille in Hollywood
Anne Frank in Amsterdam
John Fremont in San Francisco
Bruno Hauptmann in New York
Jim Jones in Guyana
J. F. Kennedy in Washington
Krishnamurti in Ojai
Louis XIV in Paris
A. S. McPherson in Los Angeles
Mies van der Rohe in Chicago
Joe Montana in San Francisco
Muhammad Ali in Zaire
Louis Pasteur in Paris
Nancy Reagan in Washington
Wm. Rehnquist in Washington
Lowell Thomas in Lhasa

JUPITER SQUARE MC

- grandiose ideas and plans
- often no funds to complete projects
- ostentatious
- loves to do things in grand fashion and damned be the cost
- little practical sense
- lack of humility
- boastful and conceited
- abundant and restless energy
- accomplishes much but also wastes talents
- selfish side surfaces every now and then in displays or arrogance or impatience
- wants it all
- sometimes takes shortcuts if necessary
- often considered a "know it all"
- could be a sycophant or bootlicker or worse
- reputation as a smart aleck
- projects an air of authority
- one's own big mouth is often your worst enemy
- gossips and badmouths others at times
- diligently searches for truth and justice
- problems with the police

Jane Addams in Chicago
Lenny Bruce in New York
Pearl Buck in Nanking
Richard Burton in Hollywood
Father Damien in Hawaii
Mme du Barry in Paris
Adolph Eichmann in Jerusalem
Elizabeth II in London
R. W. Emerson in Boston
Douglas Fairbanks in Hollywood
Clark Gable in Hollywood
Rajiv Gandhi in New Delhi
Greta Garbo in Hollywood
U. S. Grant in Washington
Hirohito in Tokyo
John Holmes in Hollywood
Mata Hari in Paris
Dan Quayle in Washington
Ronald Reagan in Hollywood
P. B. Shelley in Italy
Frank Sinatra in Hollywood
Steven Spielberg in Hollywood
Johann Strauss in Vienna

John Sutter in Sacramento
Jack Valenti in Hollywood

JUPITER TRINE MC

- constructive, conservative and traditional outlook
- favors granted by those in superior positions of power, authority or wealth
- honesty and sincerity bring success and good fortune
- professional and domestic matters couldn't be better
- likes to help others
- politics, the law or medicine favored
- willing and avid student
- mind is curious and seldom idle
- abundant energy requires many outlets
- interest in sporting events
- happy and optimistic
- nice person to have around
- hobbies could turn a profit
- loves to travel and explore
- sometimes expects too much
- basic faith in the goodness of mankind

Christiaan Barnard in Cape Town
Walter Cronkhite in New York
Marie Curie in Paris
Christian Dior in Paris
L. B. Johnson in Vietnam
Maria Theresa in Vienna
Mary I in London
Maximilian in Mexico
Bette Midler in Hollywood
Harvey Milk in San Francisco
J. P. Morgan in New York
Napoleon I on St. Helena
Sydney Omarr in Hollywood
Grace Slick in San Francisco
Tokyo Rose in Tokyo

JUPITER INCONJUNCT MC

- mixed feelings about those in power and authority
- conflict of values and whether to obey the law or follow one's own course in life
- others often try and restrict your freedom

- contacts with the police possible
- dilemma between wanting to play and the necessity of working for a living
- must sacrifice personal ambition
- often forced to serve others
- restlessness causes frequent changes of occupation or residence
- easily bored with the familiar
- continually seeks the new and unusual
- must learn to see the big picture
- often gets immersed in the details
- highly self righteous
- thinks one has all the answers
- often unwilling to listen or learn

Tsarina Alexandra in Leningrad
Edgar Cayce in Virginia Beach
Cher in Hollywood
William Gladstone in London
Joseph Goebbels in Berlin
Hermann Goering in Berlin
Adolf Hitler in Berlin
James Huberty in San Diego
Michael Jordan in Chicago
Helen Keller in New York
Helmut Kohl in Bonn
Gertrude Stein in Paris
Shirley Temple in Hollywood
Tiberius in Rome
Harry Truman in Hiroshima
Oscar Wilde in Paris

JUPITER OPPOSITE MC/CONJ IC
- good place for retirement or attaining domestic security and stability
- much comfort, ease and luxury domestically
- sometimes the head of a clan
- wants a large family
- all real estate matters favored
- wants to live in a big house
- high degree of claustrophobia
- needs space and freedom
- wants peace and tranquillity
- home is a refuge from the outside world
- strong interest in family history
- good for research and genealogy
- traditional and conventional outlook

- patriotic and chauvinistic
- interested in people from other lands, their customs, religions and food
- possibly the best place on earth in which to reside as you really feel at home here
- this is your personal Garden of Eden, your Utopia or your Nirvana

Barbara Cartland in London
Catherine the Great in Leningrad
Henry Ford II in Detroit
Ernest Hemingway in Idaho
Jack Kerouac in San Francisco
Madonna in Hollywood
Wm. McKinley in Washington
Bernard Montgomery in El Alamein
Jacqueline Onassis in Greece
Marcel Proust in Paris
Carl Sandburg in Chicago
Ted Turner in Hollywood

SATURN CONJUNCT ASC
- faced with many responsibilities, duties and obligations
- serious attitude about life which is often considered a burden
- many worries and anxieties
- difficult just to sit down and relax
- spartan and austere environment
- weak physical constitution and vitality
- a loner with few close friends
- hard to relate to strangers
- conscientious and dependable
- can always be counted on in a crisis
- may encounter periods of hunger, privation or depression
- orderly, frugal and immensely practical
- much patience and foresight
- puritanical, skeptical and reserved nature keeps others at a distance
- shy and retiring
- often inhibited and timid
- seeks seclusion
- often lonely, especially in crowds
- can be selfish and melancholic

Marlon Brando in Tahiti
Al Capone in Chicago
Jimmy Carter in Washington
Indira Gandhi in New Delhi
Goethe in Weimar
James Huberty in San Diego
John Paul II in Rome
Christine Jorgensen in Denmark
Grace Kelly in Monaco
Bette Midler in New York
Richard Nixon in Peking
Margaret Thatcher in London
Tiberius in Rome

SATURN SEXTILE ASC

- serious disposition wins support and admiration from those in authority
- reliable and responsible
- reputation is one of honesty and integrity
- good personal self discipline
- very well organized and efficient
- seemingly cold and impersonal but loyal to the nth degree
- older and serious friends favored who are mature in their basic outlook
- uncomfortable in group situations
- basic problems with communication
- good for students
- mathematical, scientific or business studies favored
- a realist who sees life for what it really is, not for what it might be someday
- impenetrable and calm
- has a paternal outlook
- young people look up to you due to your inherent wisdom and experience

Queen Anne in London
Wm. J. Bryan in Washington
Yul Brynner in Hollywood
C. B. DeMille in Hollywood
Amelia Earhart in the Howland Islands
Elizabeth II in London
F. S. Fitzgerald in Hollywood
Rajiv Gandhi in New Delhi
J. Edgar Hoover in Washington
Aldous Huxley in Hollywood

Nikita Khrushchev in Moscow
G. Gordon Liddy in Washington
Sophia Loren in Paris
Margaret Mead in Samoa
Joe Montana in San Francisco
Jacqueline Onassis in Greece
Theodore Roosevelt in Cuba

SATURN SQUARE ASC

- lack of inherent warmth and friendliness creates problems in relationships
- sour dispositions repulses strangers who find you unresponsive to their needs
- often feels unloved or unworthy
- hard to find suitable marriage partners
- needs considerable emotional support
- often places demands on others
- a perfectionist and faultfinder
- detests failure
- highly critical of self and others
- depression and insecurity causes you to retreat from unpleasantness
- lonely and alienated
- compensates for lack of love through hard work
- pessimistic, fearful and cynical
- holds others at an arm's length
- inhibited when in the public eye

Christopher Boyce in Mexico City
Ray Bradbury in Hollywood
H. G. Brown in New York
Jerry Falwell in Lynchburg
Greta Garbo in Hollywood
Giuseppe Garibaldi in Rome
Jean Genet in Paris
Katharine Hepburn in Hollywood
Rudolf Hess in Berlin
Ethel Kennedy in Washington
R. F. Kennedy in Los Angeles
Michael Landon in Hollywood
Peter Max in New York
Napoleon I on St. Helena
George Patton in Frankfurt
Joseph Wambaugh in Los Angeles

SATURN TRINE ASC
- cautious and conservative

- dignified, honest and full of integrity
- never acts in a rash or hasty manner
- gains much admiration and respect
- cooperates easily with others providing they
- measure up to your standards
- an ardent realist who believs in results
- theories are a waste of time
- good for students of math, science or medicine
- often considered dull or prosaic
- very self disciplined
- always works hard
- good organizer and an effective administrator
- good place to go into business
- puts off pleasure until the task is completed
- can always be counted upon when the chips are down

Josephine Baker in Paris
David Ben Gurion in Jerusalem
Irving Berlin in New York
Anita Bryant in Miami
Mary Baker Eddy in Boston
Bobby Fischer in Iceland
John Fremont in San Francisco
J. P. Getty in London
Arthur Godfrey in Miami
Ernest Hemingway in Idaho
Herbert Hoover in Washington
Ivan the Terrible in Moscow
Louis XVI in Paris
Shirley MacLaine in Hollywood
Nelson Mandela in Cape Town
Rupert Murdoch in New York
Pius XII in Rome
Bertrand Russell in Boston
Lowell Thomas in Lhasa
Henry Thoreau in Concord
Richard Wagner in Zurich

SATURN INCONJUNCT ASC
- very serious about life
- difficult to just sit down and relax
- responsibilities continually thrust upon one's shoulders
- many doubts about your ability to complete the assigned task or job
- many periods of self doubt or depression

- gets caught up in the details
- detests being in crowds
- prefers to spend most of the time alone
- lacks basic self confidence
- needs much emotional support and reassurance
- needs to be motivated by something other than money
- authority often questioned
- almost impossible to admit defeat, to apologize or to surrender

Prince Albert in London
Warren Beatty in Hollywood
John DeLorean in Detroit
Anne Frank in Amsterdam
Bob Geldof in Ethiopia
Henry VIII in London
L. Ron Hubbard in Los Angeles
Lee Iacocca in Detroit
Christopher Isherwood in Berlin
Douglas MacArthur in Manila
Maximilian in Mexico
Dan Rather in New York
Erwin Rommel at El Alamein
Diana Ross in Detroit
George Sand in Paris
Carl Sandburg in Chicago
Rod Serling in Hollywood
Gertrude Stein in Paris
Rudolph Valentino in Hollywood
Giuseppe Verdi in Milan

SATURN OPPOSITE ASC/CONJ DESC
- long-term relationships possible providing one is willing to wait and endure certain limitations
- marriage comes when one matures
- must learn to bend and adjust
- must accept responsibility for others
- prefers older and wiser individuals
- marriage can give one status as well as a higher income
- often builds a wall around oneself
- tendency to criticize or dominate the partner
- tries to control or manipulate the partner
- anxious about making commitments
- very high ideals and standards
- appears selective and snobbish

- highly discriminating about friends and associates
- cooperation comes with difficulty due to basic reserved nature
- many periods of dejection, rejection and denial
- could remain single and like it

Reinhard Heydrich in Berlin
Howard Hughes in Las Vegas
Shirley MacLaine in Hollywood
Muhammad Ali in Zaire
Florence Nightingale in the Crimea
Nelson Rockefeller in Washington
H. Ross Perot in Dallas
Vanna White in Hollywood
Simon Wiesenthal in Vienna

SATURN CONJUNCT MC
- possibility of rising to great heights of prominence and power
- not afraid to work long hours to insure eventual success
- an effective administrator or executive
- interested in politics and all government issues
- conservative, traditional and stable nature endears you to those in authority
- willing to forego momentary pleasure to secure one's position in life
- wants respect more than anything
- self disciplined and persistent
- could become a dictator or petty tyrant if things don't go as planned
- a true workaholic who's not interested in the social scene
- thought of as a loner or miser
- many periodic bouts of depression
- sometimes oversteps one's authority which leads to a great fall from power
- slow but difficult advancement
- often stoic, spartan and austere demeanor

Elizabeth II in London
Helmut Kohl in Bonn
Mao Tse-tung in Peking
Napoleon in Paris
George Patton in Frankfurt
Mme de Pompadour in Paris

Shah of Iran in Teheran
Norman Schwarzkopf in Kuwait
Oscar Wilde in Paris
Boris Yeltsin in Moscow

SATURN SEXTILE MC
- professional and domestic life is stable and well ordered
- much foresight, patience, discipline and persistence
- willing to cooperate and play the game by the rules
- systematic and organized
- highly conventional and traditional
- family life is important
- may follow a parental vocation
- prefers to work alone or with someone who is older and wiser
- dependable, trustworthy and responsible
- handles a crisis with little emotion
- patiently pursues one's ambition
- often self absorbed and selfish
- relentless and plodding
- never loses sight of the eventual goal

Konrad Adenauer in Bonn
Melvin Belli in San Francisco
Lizzie Borden in Fall River
Pearl Buck in Nanking
Al Capone in Chicago
Cellini in Florence
Captain Cook in Sydney
Edward VII in London
Douglas Fairbanks in Hollywood
Errol Flynn in Hollywood
Diane von Furstenburg in New York
Che Guevara in Havana
Dag Hammarksjold in New York
Haydn in Vienna
Lee Iacocca in Detroit
Jim Jones in Guyana
Christine Jorgensen in Denmark
Grace Kelly in Monaco
Rudyard Kipling in London
Charles Manson in Los Angeles
Richard Nixon in Washington
Oliver North in Washington

Yoko Ono in New York
Edith Piaf in Paris
Tom Selleck in Honolulu
Rod Serling in Hollywood
Tiberius in Rome
Pierre Trudeau in Ottawa
George Washington in Philadelphia

SATURN SQUARE MC

- burdens and responsibilities limit both success and happiness
- relations with others fraught with tension and stress
- parents place burdens on one's shoulders
- homelife is seldom happy
- prefers to be left alone
- hard to relate with strangers
- others think you're cold and impersonal
- often downright hard and cruel
- very sensitive to other's opinions
- too shy or timid to show them how you really feel
- lacks basic self confidence
- has strong inferiority complex
- must continually prove oneself
- gets little positive feedback
- finds it hard to make new friends
- pessimistic and doubting
- fear about one's position in life or job security

Ingrid Bergman in Rome
Rosa Bonheur in Paris
Van Cliburn in Moscow
Marion Davies in Hollywood
Enrico Fermi in Chicago
Indira Gandhi in New Delhi
Bruno Hauptmann in New York
Hirohito in Tokyo
Xaviera Hollander in New York
Howard Hughes in Las Vegas
Carl Jung in Zurich
Ted Kennedy in Washington
Rupert Murdoch in London
Benito Mussolini in Rome
Florence Nightingale in the Crimea
Roman Polanski in Hollywood
John Steinbeck in Salinas

Adlai Stevenson in New York
Shirley Temple in Hollywood
Jack Valenti in Hollywood
Earl Warren in Washington
Simon Wiesenthal in Vienna

SATURN TRINE MC

- goals easy to reach
- usually realizes one's ambition
- likes to work hard as one is not a clock watcher
- slow but steady climb to the top
- dependable and reliable nature wins points with the boss
- a workaholic
- very well organized
- likes order but hates change
- prefers company of mature individuals who are serious about life
- a perfectionist
- prefers to work alone
- systematic and plodding
- few measure up to your very high standards or ideals
- always trustworthy and honest
- hates being the center of attention
- not out for a popularity contest

Jim Bakker in Charlotte
Cher in Hollywood
Father Damien in Hawaii
Gerald Ford in Washington
Henry Ford II in Detroit
M. K. Gandhi in New Delhi
George Gershwin in Hollywood
Ernest Hemingway in Paris
D. H. Lawrence in Taos
Sophia Loren in Paris
Douglas MacArthur in Manila
Jacqueline Onassis in Washington
Babe Ruth in New York
Carl Sandburg in Chicago
Edith Wilson in Washington
Brigham Young in Salt Lake City

SATURN INCONJUNCT MC

- feels lonely and isolated most of the time
- a loner and miser at heart

- wants to impress others but has few opportunities for recognition
- needs love and respect from intimates
- wants admiration from those in power
- continually searching for a father figure
- finds it hard to take orders
- prefers to work rather than play
- finds it hard to sit down and relax
- life is well structured with little room for expansion or adventure
- strict and spartan desires
- places limits on oneself and surroundings
- minds one's own business
- wants to be free from burdens or responsibilities
- trouble finding suitable employment
- long periods of depression or penury

Theodore Bundy in Seattle
Richard Burton in Hollywood
George Bush in Washington
Frederic Chopin in Paris
Jean Genet in Paris
Joseph Goebbels in Berlin
John Holmes in Hollywood
Louis XIV in Paris
Mies van der Rohe in Chicago
Joe Montana in San Francisco
Sydney Omarr in Hollywood
Aristotle Onassis in Buenos Aires
Prince Philip in London
Elvis Presley in Memphis
Bertrand Russell in Boston
Ken Uston in Las Vegas
Rudolph Valentino in New York
Orson Welles in Hollywood

SATURN OPPOSITE MC/CONJ IC
- domestic and homelife likely to be quite cold and formal
- traditional and conservative family background
- likes to be the boss at home and demands respect
- relations with parents are distant and problematic
- many burdens in early life
- often finds it hard to live up to parental ideals or standards

- conflict between professional and domestic concerns
- should consider having an office in the home
- often lonely and isolated
- needs much emotional support and reassurance
- projects an aura of self sufficiency
- may become a hermit or miser
- values neatness and order
- surroundings are spartan and austere
- buys for practicality
- little room for the frills of life

Barbara Cartland in London
James Dean in Hollywood
Christian Dior in Paris
L. Ron Hubbard in Los Angeles
Ivan the Terrible in Moscow
John XXIII in Rome
Horatio Nelson at Trafalgar
Nicholas II in Leningrad
Cecil Rhodes in Rhodesia
Meryl Streep in Hollywood
Barbra Streisand in Hollywood

URANUS CONJUNCT ASC
- known as a free spirit
- highly unconventional, eccentric and rebellious
- loves to challenge tradition and authority
- plays the role of the devil's advocate
- likes to keep things stirred up
- easily bored and restless
- high strung and nervous
- impatience may cause accidents or injuries
- life fluctuates from one unexpected event to another
- very unpredictable
- possibility of danger or violence
- much excitement and adventure
- very progressive and open minded
- tolerant of others but demands personal freedom
- likes anyone or anything that's weird, odd or unusual
- affinity for the funky or kinky
- often erratic, undependable and scattered
- always abrupt and outspoken

Ansel Adams in Yosemite
Isadora Duncan in Nice
Henry Ford II in Detroit
Clark Gable in Hollywood
Bruno Hauptmann in New York
Charles Lindbergh in New York
Alice R. Longworth in Washington
Maximilian in Mexico
George Patton in Frankfurt
Juan Peron in Buenos Aires
Dan Quayle in Washington
F. D. Roosevelt in Washington
Gloria Swanson in Hollywood
Stanford White in New York

William Gladstone in London
Heinrich Himmler in Berlin
Herbert Hoover in Washington
Rudyard Kipling in London
Douglas MacArthur in Manila
John McEnroe in London
Nelson Mandela in Johannesburg
Benito Mussolini in Rome
Nicholas II in Leningrad
Oliver North in Washington
Yoko Ono in New York
Mary Pickford in Hollywood
Mother Teresa in Calcutta
Gloria Vanderbilt in New York

URANUS SEXTILE ASC

- peculiar ideas about life which often upset others
- highly opinionated
- outspoken and independent
- needs excitement and stimulation continually
- finds it easy to make friends
- shies away from making commitments
- needs a great deal of personal freedom
- accepts few responsibilities
- unusual lifestyle, attire or hairstyle makes one the center of attention
- can always be relied upon to do or say the unexpected
- loves to shock others
- highly romantic but little stability in love affairs
- prone towards separation or living apart
- likes anything new or original
- demands change and variety
- highly inventive and creative
- known as a futurist
- has complete lack of materialism

Boris Becker in London
Helen Gurley Brown in New York
Carol Burnett in Hollywood
Joan Crawford in Hollywood
Bette Davis in Hollywood
C. B. DeMille in Hollywood
Eamon de Valera in Dublin
Amelia Earhart in the Howland Islands
Douglas Fairbanks in Hollywood
M. K. Gandhi in Johannesburg

URANUS SQUARE ASC

- undisciplined nature flits from one thing to another
- many spasmodic disruptions in daily life
- fails to set long term goals
- highly independent and individualistic
- a nonconformist and rebel
- tries to be unique or original
- impossible to take orders from anyone in power or authority
- intimate relations fraught with tension and stress
- refuses to compromise
- very stubborn and opinionated
- watch out for injuries or accidents
- does exactly the opposite of what's expected just to prove one is in complete command
- marches to the beat of a different drummer
- a true pioneer who shocks
- inconstant and changeable
- often rude and irritable

Lenny Bruce in New York
Walter Cronkhite in New York
Tom Dooley in Laos
Edward VII in London
Frederick the Great in Berlin
George V in London
Goethe in Weimar
Gen. Gordon in the Sudan
Che Guevara in Havana
Haydn in Vienna
Stacy Keach in London

Helen Keller in New York
Krishnamurti in Ojai
Bruce Lee in Hong Kong
Machiavelli in Florence
J. Nehru in New Delhi
Nero in Rome
Manuel Noriega in Panama
Marcel Proust in Paris
Nelson Rockefeller in Washington
Lillian Russell in New York
Tiberius in Rome
Mark Twain in Hartford
Lech Walesa in Danzig
Orson Welles in Hollywood
Duke of Windsor in Paris

URANUS TRINE ASC

- unique, original and unconventional lifestyle is admired by others
- abundant willpower and high degree of creativity
- sparks enthusiasm in others and gains support of those in power
- won't be controlled or restricted in any way
- highly independent
- learns best from experience
- finds it difficult to study from books
- inventive nature loves to challenge the status quo
- shocks others but in an inoffensive manner
- very intuitive and psychic
- interested in the unusual or offbeat
- dynamic and charismatic personality
- excited by anything new and unusual

Marlon Brando in Hollywood
Yul Brynner in Hollywood
Carol Channing in New York
Captain Cook in Sydney
Father Damien in Hawaii
Deng Xiaoping in Peking
Mme du Barry in Paris
Bobby Fischer in Iceland
Gerald Ford in Washington
Galileo in Rome
Antonio Gaudi in Barcelona
U. S. Grant in Vicksburg
Theodor Herzl in Vienna
John XXIII in Rome

Michael Jordan in Chicago
Timothy Leary in San Francisco
Vivien Leigh in Hollywood
Nikolai Lenin in Moscow
David Lloyd George in London
Roman Polanski in Hollywood
Mme de Pompadour in Paris
Shirley Temple in Hollywood
Rudolph Valentino in New York
Earl Warren in Washington

URANUS INCONJUNCT ASC

- restricted from being as free and independent as one desires
- unusual or unexpected occurrences deter one from the original gameplan
- frequent crises develop at a moment's notice
- must remain flexible and learn to adapt
- hard to release physical or emotional tension
- frequent outbursts of anger
- hates routine or repetition
- easily bored with little capacity for concentration
- pathological need to be free and uncommitted
- totally unpredictable and erratic
- often confuses others as to one's intent
- often rash and compulsive
- possibility of violence or accidents
- goes against the grain most of the time
- is usually "out of sync"
- often pulled in two directions at once
- periodic indecision or vacillation

John Barrymore in Hollywood
Cellini in Florence
James Dean in Hollywood
Charles de Gaulle in Paris
D. D. Eisenhower in Washington
J. P. Getty in London
Whoopi Goldberg in Hollywood
Cary Grant in Hollywood
Anver Joffrey in New York
Marie of Romania in Bucharest
Wm. McKinley in Washington
Prince Philip in London
Ronald Reagan in Managua
R. L. Stevenson in Samoa

URANUS OPPOSITE ASC/CONJ DESC

- compulsive need for freedom and independence in relationships
- needs tons of tolerance and understanding
- shuns intimacy or close emotional contacts
- falls "in love" quite easily
- highly romantic and idealistic
- seldom sticks around long enough for others to really get to know you
- wants to be as free as the wind
- uncommitted to anyone or anyplace
- attracted to oddballs, weirdos and eccentrics
- unstable and unpredictable in close relationships
- won't take orders from anyone
- needs constant change and excitement
- highly sexual and often promiscuous
- highly impersonal and aloof
- like a rolling stone which gathers no moss

Indira Gandhi in New Delhi
Xaviera Hollander in New York
John Paul II in Rome
Louis XVI in Paris
Mozart in Vienna
Napoleon I in Moscow
Elizabeth Taylor in Rome
Leon Trotsky in Mexico City
Ted Turner in Hollywood
Richard Wagner in Bayreuth

URANUS CONJUNCT MC

- an individualist who always insists on doing things their own way
- resists pressure to conform
- hates convention or tradition
- always contrary, rebellious and headstrong
- nervous disorders cause anxiety
- always original and unique
- a humanitarian who wants to aid others
- strong spirit of entrepreneurship
- interested in science and technology
- creative and inventive
- ideas and projects often shock or alarm others
- frequent desire to change jobs or residence
- always searching for the ideal
- should be self employed
- has problems taking orders

- exciting but unstable lifestyle
- usually rebellious or anarchial
- sudden and unexpected turns of fate
- life here is like a roller coaster

Boris Becker in London
Chiang Kaishek in Taiwan
William Gladstone in London
Merv Griffin in Hollywood
Heinrich Himmler in Berlin
Bruce Lee in Hong Kong
Charles Lindbergh in Paris
Rupert Murdoch in London
Richard Nixon in Peking
Lillian Russell in New York
Robert Schumann in Leipzig

URANUS SEXTILE MC

- gains support and assistance from those who appreciate your originality
- high degree of creativity
- many talents gain attention and admiration
- easy to make important social and business contacts
- interest in the humanities, science, technology, astrology or the occult
- doesn't feel obligated by tradition or convention
- a social pioneer
- needs freedom and privacy
- hates to make commitments
- feels different from others but not alienated from humanity
- works well alone or with others
- has learned to be tolerant and understanding
- tries to be cooperative
- always self assertive and decisive
- very dynamic and charismatic
- lucky in career matters
- fortunate turns for the better most of the time

Ingrid Bergman in Rome
Mme du Barry in Paris
Enrico Fermi in Chicago
Hirohito in Tokyo
Victor Hugo in Paris
Anver Joffrey in New York
Lafayette in Philadelphia

Mies van der Rohe in Chicago
Audie Murphy in France
Lee Harvey Oswald in Dallas
Ronald Reagan in Washington
Artur Rubinstein in New York
George Sand in Paris
Diana Spencer in London
R. L. Stevenson in Samoa
Richard Wagner in Bayreuth

URANUS SQUARE MC
- cannot and will not conform to conventional standards
- a true rebel or revolutionary
- responsibilities and obligations and either forgotten or ignored completely
- rebels against anyone in power or authority
- can't take direction or orders
- changes jobs and residence capriciously
- can't settle down to anyone or anything for too long
- likes being the "black sheep"
- a real eccentric, oddball or weirdo
- always does the exact opposite of what's expected
- perverse nature requires using reverse psychology
- totally unpredictable, unreliable and irresponsible
- very moody and temperamental
- stubborn and uncompromising
- loves to shock others
- very independent
- frequent domestic or professional upsets

Ann Margret in Hollywood
John Belushi in Hollywood
Sir Richard Burton in Mecca
Cher in Hollywood
Marion Davies in Hollywood
Charles de Gaulle in Paris
Sigmund Freud in Vienna
J. P. Getty in London
Helmut Kohl in Bonn
Alice R. Longworth in Washington
J. P. Morgan in New York
Aristotle Onassis in Buenos Aires
George Patton in Frankfurt

Peter the Great in Leningrad
Bhagwan Rajneesh in Oregon
F. D. Roosevelt in Washington
Diana Ross in Detroit
Wm. H. Taft in Washington
Lowell Thomas in Lhasa
Ken Uston in Las Vegas
Duchess of Windsor in London

URANUS TRINE MC
- original and unusual ideas and beliefs
- places a different value on things
- hates being tied down
- seldom accumulates possessions or security
- follows a unique path in life
- seldom has to battle those in power
- quietly independent
- highly creative and inventive
- overly impatient
- loves excitement and craves stimulation
- easily bored with routine
- oriented towards the future
- unique contribution to society
- interested in science and technology
- a true humanitarian at heart
- makes friends easily
- good for politicians or those involved in social work

Konrad Adenauer in Bonn
Honore de Balzac in Paris
Bartholdi in New York
Michael Bennett in New York
Elizabeth II in London
Eugenie in Paris
Greta Garbo in Hollywood
Dag Hammarksjold in New York
Rudolf Hess in Berlin
Charlton Heston in Hollywood
Reinhard Heydrich in Berlin
Imelda Marcos in Manila
Jacqueline Onassis in Greece
Robert Redford in Utah
John Steinbeck in Salinas
Meryl Streep in Hollywood
Vincent van Gogh in Arles
Voltaire in Paris

URANUS INCONJUNCT MC

- easily irritated and agitated when others are in too close proximity
- often shocks or offends others
- creates situations which upset the status quo or basic equilibrium
- difficulty relating to anyone who gets too intimate or tries to direct events
- hates being told what to do or how to act
- highly perverse and stubborn
- often disregards advice
- seldom listens to one's conscience
- frequent crises upset domestic or professional peace
- needs encouragement and self confidence
- demands freedom and independence
- should be self employed
- often a futurist
- visions and creative talents often go unnoticed or unappreciated
- out of time and out of place

Tsarina Alexandra in Leningrad
Gloria Allred in Los Angeles
Jim Bakker in Charlotte
Bismarck in Berlin
Ray Bradbury in Hollywood
Barbara Cartland in London
Father Damien in Hawaii
Bob Geldof in Ethiopia
Jesse Helms in Washington
Ernest Hemingway in Idaho
Jim Jones in Guyana and San Francisco
J. F. Kennedy in Washington
Vivien Leigh in Hollywood
Liberace in Las Vegas
Martin Luther in Wittenberg
Billy Martin in New York
Bernard Montgomery in El Alamein
Rudolph Nureyev in New York
Edith Piaf in Paris
Elvis Presley in Memphis
Wm. Rehnquist in Washington
Father Serra in San Diego
Harry Truman in Hiroshima

URANUS OPPOSITE MC/CONJ IC

- domestic situation or lifestyle constantly changes from one day to the next
- little stability or security
- wants a modern home with all the latest gadgets
- home may be headquarters for some type of group activity or club
- relations with parents fraught with tension or stress
- often runs away from home
- wants to be free from having to obey orders at home
- a true individualist
- needs complete freedom of motion and thought
- can't tolerate displays of emotion or jealousy
- won't be possessed or controlled
- hates to be cuddled or touched
- likes to remain aloof and impersonal
- home life or family tradition mean little
- likes to keep things simple or spartan
- evades or ignores responsibilities
- little sense of being rooted to a place
- a natural wanderer
- the family's "black sheep"
- a true original

Frederic Chopin in Paris
Eamon de Valera in Dublin
Thomas Edison in Menlo Park
George V in London
Haydn in Vienna
Ernest Hemingway in Havana
Nelson Mandela in Cape Town
Nelson Rockefeller in Washington
Barbra Streisand in Hollywood

NEPTUNE CONJUNCT ASC

- retreats from the harsh realities of life
- creates one's own personal paradise
- powerful imagination and intuition
- strong psychic powers
- confusion between reality and illusion
- lives in a fantasy world
- vulnerable and impressionable
- lets others walk all over you
- sometimes a masochist
- must learn to stand on one's own feet

- can't rely on others for support
- possible contact with criminal types or the police
- can be a dangerous place to reside
- can escape unpleasantness through drugs or alcohol
- sometimes uses bad judgment
- often feels unloved or unworthy
- has low self esteem
- should become involved with spiritual movements
- sensitive to noise
- turned on by art, beauty or music
- can be gullible and deceived by others
- very insecure and misguided
- tries to be gentle, kind and sympathetic
- wants to help those less fortunate

James Dean in Hollywood
Benjamin Disraeli in London
Bobby Fischer in Iceland
J. P. Getty in London
Francisco Goya in Madrid
Louis XIV in Paris
Josef Mengele in Auschwitz
Prince Philip in London
Marcel Proust in Paris
Ronald Reagan in Washington
Andy Warhol in New York
Dan White in San Francisco

NEPTUNE SEXTILE ASC
- extremely sensitive to the needs and wants of the public
- goes out of the way to help or assist
- can't endure suffering or pain in others
- periodic visions and strong psychic hunches foresee the future
- lives in a fantasy world
- idealistic, magnetic and charismatic
- compassionate and understanding
- great deal of sympathy and compassion
- attracted to the mysteries of life
- involvement with the spirit world
- has an aura of refinement and culture
- attracted to artists, musicians or actors
- highly romantic
- difficult to separate fact from fiction

- sees life through rose colored glasses

Alexander Bell in Boston
Fidel Castro in Havana
Catherine the Great in Leningrad
Eamon de Valera in Dublin
Walt Disney in Hollywood
Tom Dooley in Laos
Ralph Waldo Emerson in Boston
Jerry Falwell in Lynchburg
Douglas Fairbanks in Hollywood
Galileo in Rome
Xaviera Hollander in New York
J. F. Kennedy in Dallas
Krishnamurti in Ojai
Machiavelli in Florence
Francois Mitterand in Paris
Napoleon I in Moscow
Christina Onassis in Greece
Jacqueline Onassis in Dallas
Pius XII in Rome
Nancy Reagan in Washington
Anwar Sadat in Cairo
Leon Trotsky in Mexico City
Pierre Trudeau in Ottawa
Stanford White in New York

NEPTUNE SQUARE ASC
- must be completely honest and aboveboard to avoid misunderstandings
- scandal often threatens the reputation
- many don't trust your motives
- tends to exaggerate the facts
- can be suspicious or paranoid
- considerable sacrifice required
- possible martyrdom or imprisonment
- very dependent on others for one's self image
- often unreliable or fuzzy perceptions
- susceptible to drugs or alcohol
- often betrayed by former friends or associates
- dishonest or fraudulent business dealings
- tends to be an escapist
- very moody and temperamental
- appears confused, weak or disappointed
- could end up living on welfare or public aid
- always seeks the ideal
- fascination for music, movies and the arts

Brigitte Bardot in Paris
Christopher Boyce in Mexico City
Johannes Brahms in Vienna
Marlon Brando in Hollywood
Ted Bundy in Seattle
Mother Cabrini in New York
Cher in Hollywood
Father Damien in Hawaii
John Dillinger in Chicago
Walt Disney in Orlando
Mamie Eisenhower in Washington
Elizabeth I in London
Jane Fonda in Hollywood
Franz Ferdinand in Sarajevo
James A. Garfield in Washington
Arthur Godfrey in Miami
Haydn in Vienna
Lady Bird Johnson in Washington
Jim Jones in San Francisco
Christine Jorgensen in Denmark
Lafayette in Philadelphia
Michael Landon in Hollywood
Horatio Nelson at Trafalgar
Richard Nixon in Washington
Rudolph Nureyev in New York
George Patton in Frankfurt
Pablo Picasso in Paris
Elvis Presley in Memphis
Mme de Pompadour in Paris
Nelson Rockefeller in Washington
Norman Schwarzkopf in Kuwait
Gloria Vanderbilt in New York
Voltaire in Paris
Joseph Wambaugh in Los Angeles

NEPTUNE TRINE ASC
- vivid imagination and high degree of intuition
- a psychic sponge
- an ardent idealist
- extremely sensitive
- completely unselfish
- always gives more than one hopes to receive
- can be self sacrificing
- wants to teach others about the mysteries of life
- spiritually motivated
- a creative genius
- high degree of inspiration which gains publicity

- others appreciate your uniqueness
- strong and magnetic personality
- attracts people who inspire you to reach your highest potential
- an aura of glamour and illusion
- favored for those in movies, music or the arts

Josephine Baker in Paris
David Ben Gurion in Jerusalem
Bismarck in Berlin
Martin Bormann in Berlin
Lenny Bruce in New York
Mary Cassatt in Paris
Edgar Cayce in Virginia Beach
Richard Chamberlain in London
Chiang Kaishek in Taiwan
Joan Crawford in Hollywood
Christian Dior in Paris
Phil Donahue in Hollywood
Gerald Ford in San Francisco
Giuseppe Garibaldi in Rome
John XXIII in Rome
Grace Kelly in Monaco
Ted Kennedy in Washington
R. F. Kennedy in Washington
Martin Luther King in Memphis
Groucho Marx in Hollywood
Bette Midler in Hollywood
Harvey Milk in San Francisco
Johann Strauss in Vienna
Tchaikowsky in Leningrad
Mother Teresa in Calcutta

NEPTUNE INCONJUNCT ASC
- must learn to make sacrifices willingly in order to achieve goals
- often yields to outside pressure
- often the unwitting victim or martyr
- hidden resentment surfaces when you fail to stand up for your rights
- often forced to be a teacher or role model
- others need sympathy or compassion
- overly sensitive to the environment
- hard to diagnose illnesses or diseases
- very impressionable or gullible
- soaks up vibrations like a sponge
- sometimes a hypochondriac

- should stay away from drugs or booze
- periodically avoids reality
- escapes into a fantasy world
- often involved in scandals
- reputation could suffer
- possibility of name changes

Helena Blavatsky in London
Winston Churchill in London
Marion Davies in Hollywood
Elizabeth II in London
M. K. Gandhi in Johannesburg
U. S. Grant in Washington
Katharine Hepburn in Hollywood
John Paul I in Rome
Juan Carlos in Madrid
Stacy Keach in London
Nikolai Lenin in Moscow
Juan Peron in Buenos Aires
Mary Pickford in Hollywood
Carroll Righter in Hollywood
Richard Wagner in Zurich
Edith Wilson in Washington

NEPTUNE OPPOSITE ASC/CONJ DESC
- often feels disappointed and confused about intimate relationships
- often deceived, dejected or abused
- attracts flakes or parasites
- idealistic, impressionable and gullible
- seeks to mold others into one's sense of perfection
- places loved ones on a pedestal
- sees others through rose colored glasses
- often gives up and lets others take the lead
- can play the role of a martyr
- unrealistic expectations in love and romance
- attracted to artistic or musical types
- wants creative and refined partners
- often forced to take care of others
- must sacrifice personal desires

Irving Berlin in New York
Capt. Bligh in Tahiti
Al Capone in Chicago
Catherine of Aragon in London
Phil Donahue in New York

Bob Fosse in New York
Hirohito in Tokyo
Aldous Huxley in Los Angeles
R. F. Kennedy in Los Angeles
Douglas MacArthur in Manila
Charles Manson in Los Angeles
Leontyne Price in New York
Gavrilo Princip in Sarajevo
Albert Schweitzer in Gabon
Giuseppe Verdi in Milan

NEPTUNE CONJUNCT MC
- many opportunities for success in the musical or artistic world
- always the danger of apathy, laziness or confusion
- threat of scandal and loss of reputation
- often discouraged or depressed when trying to separate illusion from reality
- strong psychic intuition
- knows what the public wants in advance
- prefers to live in a fantasy world
- aura of mystery or glamour
- must sacrifice personal ambition to work for a higher cause
- often manipulated like a puppet
- seeks the ideal or utopian
- overly indecisive and vacillating
- could be involved with religion, social work or politics
- danger of escape into the world of drugs or alcohol
- wants the impossible
- possible involvement with criminal types or the police with danger of arrest or imprisonment
- exalted notion of self importance
- self deceptive or deluded about one's purpose in life

Yul Brynner in Hollywood
Mary Cassatt in Paris
Carol Channing in New York
Leonardo da Vinci in Florence
Walt Disney in Orlando
Arthur Godfrey in Miami
G. Gordon Liddy in Washington
Abraham Lincoln in Washington

Machiavelli in Florence
Richard Nixon in Washington
Nelson Rockefeller in Washington
Kaiser Wilhelm II in Berlin

NEPTUNE SEXTILE ASC
- prefers to live in a world that's peaceful and harmonious
- turned on by fantasy
- always seeks the ideal or impossible
- lacks self assertion
- picks up vibrations like a sponge
- involved with religion or spiritualism
- sensitive to music and color
- often shy and retiring
- avoids conflict from fear of being hurt or rejected
- exerts subtle power
- ability to read other's minds
- interested in the occult
- responsive, selfless and sentimental
- appears otherworldly or mystical
- tries to help others attain their goals
- great power of persuasion

Boris Becker in London
Pablo Casals in San Juan
Catherine of Aragon in London
Joan Collins in Hollywood
Eamon de Valera in Dublin
Jackie Gleason in Miami
W. R. Hearst in San Francisco
Reinhard Heydrich in Berlin
John Holmes in Hollywood
L. Ron Hubbard in Los Angeles
L. B. Johnson in Washington
Michael Jordan in Chicago
Grace Kelly in Monaco
Liberace in Las Vegas
Louis XVI in Paris
Maximilian in Mexico
J. P. Morgan in New York
Mozart in Vienna
Grace Slick in San Francisco
Barbra Streisand in Hollywood
Giuseppe Verdi in Milan
Barbara Walters in New York

NEPTUNE SQUARE MC
- needs to be around positive types to reinforce one's self confidence
- often self doubting and insecure
- runs away from any sign of unpleasantness
- considerable anxiety about domestic or professional matters
- confused and worried about psychic visions or hunches
- often misinterpreted or misunderstood
- possibility of scandal, arrest or confinement in a hospital, asylum or prison
- must learn to keep one's feet on the ground
- learn to separate fact from fiction
- steer clear of drugs and alcohol
- can be involved with criminal types
- messy and disorganized environment
- back lack of efficiency or system
- can be lazy and disinterested
- easily deceived
- many misguided notions
- hypersensitive to the environment
- possibility of mental illness
- inferiority complex

Capt. Bligh in Tahiti
Enrico Caruso in New York
James Dean in Hollywood
Elizabeth II in London
Bobby Fischer in Iceland
Frederick the Great in Berlin
Bruno Hauptmann in New York
Hindenburg in Berlin
Anver Joffrey in New York
Jack London in the Yukon
Douglas MacArthur in Manila
Yoko Ono in New York
P. B. Shelley in Italy
Andy Warhol in New York

NEPTUNE TRINE MC
- wants to escape into a world of illusion and fantasy
- possibility of scandal
- non materialistic outlook with few possessions
- wants to be as free as a bird
- values emotions more than things

- will literally give the shirt off one's back
- completely unselfish
- always trying to help those down on their luck
- reserved and shy around strangers
- feelings are easily hurt
- a devoted friend who willingly makes sacrifices
- anticipates what the boss or the public wants
- uncanny knack for reading minds
- life is often lived on a spiritual plane
- interested in the supernatural

John Barrymore in Hollywood
Warren Beatty in Hollywood
Michael Bennett in New York
D. D. Eisenhower in Washington
Jane Fonda in Hanoi
Henry Ford II in Detroit
Diane von Furstenburg in New York
J. P. Getty in London
Gary Hart in Miami
Theodor Herzl in Vienna
Don Johnson in Miami
Ethel Kennedy in Washington
Ferdinand Marcos in Manila
Joe Montana in San Francisco
Nero in Rome
Robespierre in Paris
Lowell Thomas in Lhasa
Henry Thoreau in Concord
Rudolph Valentino in Hollywood
Lech Walesa in Danzig
Duchess of Windsor in London

NEPTUNE INCONJUNCT MC
- necessity of fortifying one's self confidence
- questions one's ability or worth
- often yields to those in power or authority
- easy to control or manipulate
- unclear about basic mission in life
- often just "goes with the flow"
- high degree of intuition and circumspection
- periodic bouts of depression
- very high standards or ideals which outsiders seldom match
- lack of foresight may cause arrest or imprisonment

possibility of living on welfare or being given up for adoption
- must make continual sacrifices
- retreats into a dream world
- could enter a monastery or convent
- turned on by religion or music

Prince Albert in London
Lord Byron in Greece
Ted Bundy in Seattle
Adolph Eichmann in Berlin
R. W. Emerson in Boston
Errol Flynn in Hollywood
Gerald Ford in San Francisco
Anne Frank in Amsterdam
Sigmund Freud in Vienna
Rupert Murdoch in New York
Audie Murphy in France
Edward R. Murrow in London
Tokyo Rose in Tokyo
Yogananda in Los Angeles
Brigham Young in Salt Lake City

NEPTUNE OPPOSITE MC/CONJ IC
- home life must be completely peaceful and serene
- needs to retreat from the outside world
- sensitive to hidden energies within the earth
- irritated by noise or loud music
- easily upset if things go wrong
- can't deal with pressure or stress
- family mysteries surface
- possibility of adoption
- susceptible to drugs or alcohol
- places parents on a pedestal
- interested in family history and genealogy
- finds skeletons in the closet
- known as the "black sheep" of the clan
- dependent on others for survival
- could live on welfare or public assistance
- vivid imagination creates a gap between fiction and fantasy
- mentally isolated from the masses
- prefers living near water
- sensitive to various weather rhythms and fluctuations

Prince Charles in London
Father Damien in Hawaii
John Dillinger in Chicago
James A. Garfield in Washington
Judy Garland in Hollywood
A. S. McPherson in Los Angeles
Madonna in Hollywood
Bette Midler in New York
William Penn in Philadelphia
Richard I in Jerusalem
Erwin Rommel in El Alamein
Elizabeth Taylor in Hollywood
Robert Urich in Las Vegas
Orson Welles in Hollywood

PLUTO CONJUNCT ASC
- approaches life with intensity
- very compulsive and obsessive
- alternately constructive and destructive
- does nothing in moderation
- life goes from one extreme to the other
- volcanic emotions periodically erupt
- many psychological changes
- wants control of one's destiny
- wants power and authority
- danger of violence, coercion or brute force
- secretive yet overly competitive
- highly sexed and often uses one's body as a weapon or lure
- known as a loner
- seldom seeks the advice or company of others
- others feel threatened by you
- appears overpowering or intimidating
- forced to be controlled or repressed
- much inhibition and suffering
- often puts oneself at risk
- continually defies the odds
- many traumatic experiences
- life is a battle for survival
- seeks to purge or eliminate things or people from time to time
- sometimes ruthless, tyrannical or egocentric
- unscrupulous, merciless and cruel

Clara Barton in Washington
Adolph Eichmann in Jerusalem
J. P. Getty in London

Merv Griffin in Hollywood
James Madison in Washington
Ferdinand Marcos in Manila
Mary I in London
Edward R. Murrow in London
Oliver North in Washington
Christina Onassis in Greece
J. D. Rockefeller in Cleveland
Duke of Wellington at Waterloo

PLUTO SEXTILE ASC
- everyday contacts are intense
- many traumatic and dramatic changes
- finds it hard to form casual relationships
- very serious and purposeful
- magnetic and charismatic personality
- penetrating insight with the power to heal
- drawn to those who need psychological help
- gives advice and counsel freely
- involved with community projects
- interested in politics
- fantastic power of concentration
- strong self discipline
- decisive and authoritative
- driving ambition
- wants power over one's environment
- compelling and magnetic
- great power of influence
- good for propaganda

Fatty Arbuckle in Hollywood
Tsarina Alexandra in Leningrad
Rosalynn Carter in Washington
Mary Cassatt in Paris
Charles Chaplin in Hollywood
D. D. Eisenhower in London
Bobby Fischer in Iceland
William Gladstone in London
U. S. Grant in Washington
Ernest Hemingway in Idaho
Reinhard Heydrich in Berlin
John Paul II in Rome
L. B. Johnson in Washington
Bette Midler in Hollywood
Audie Murphy in France
Rupert Murdoch in New York
Napoleon I in Moscow and Cairo

Napoleon III in Paris
Cecil Rhodes in Rhodesia
Oral Roberts in Tulsa
Robespierre in Paris
Richard Wagner in Zurich
Dan White in San Francisco

PLUTO SQUARE ASC
- hard to be open, candid or direct
- secretive, unscrupulous, underhanded and sneaky
- always intense, serious and brooding
- very ambitious about one's mission in life
- refuses to compromise
- stubborn to the nth degree
- unwilling to bend or listen
- aggressive and antisocial
- violence and coercion used to gain power
- life is often placed in jeopardy by those who want to control or dominate you
- conflict over possessions and money
- sometimes gets caught with the hand in the till
- wants complete power and control over others
- autocratic, dictatorial and tyrannical
- repulsive and brutish behavior offends others
- overbearing and intimidating
- can be cruel and brutal at times
- drastic and dramatic changes in lifestyle
- highly sexed with compulsive need for physical activity
- possibility of nymphomania or satyriasis

John DeLorean in Detroit
Mary Baker Eddy in Boston
Gerald Ford in San Francisco
Frederick the Great in Berlin
Charlton Heston in Hollywood
J. F. Kennedy in Dallas
Vivien Leigh in Hollywood
F. de Lesseps in Suez
Charles Lindbergh in Paris
Francois Mitterand in Paris
Lord Mountbatten in New Delhi
Mozart in Vienna
Pat Nixon in Washington
William Penn in Philadelphia
Anwar Sadat in Cairo

Rod Serling in Hollywood
Father Serra in California
Elizabeth Taylor in Rome
Tokyo Rose in Tokyo
Pierre Trudeau in Ottawa

PLUTO TRINE ASC
- intense, serious and dedicated nature works well with and for the masses
- prefers to be left alone
- must know something in depth before commitment
- could pry and interfere
- penetrating insight
- wants to remake and reform
- keen awareness and high degree of concentration
- good for research and investigation
- good leader and organizer
- great physical strength and self confidence
- iron will makes one a force with which to be reckoned
- highly magnetic and compellingly charismatic
- usually gets one's own way or else
- sexual encounters and passionate and life changing
- frequent bouts of ecstasy
- great creative power
- can inspire the masses
- great measure of influence
- good for propagandists

Catherine of Aragon in London
A. G. Bell in Boston
Yul Brynner in Hollywood
Cellini in Florence
Charles I in London
Leonardo da Vinci in Florence
Thomas Edison in Menlo Park
Edward VII in London
M. K. Gandhi in Johannesburg
Antonio Gaudi in Barcelona
James Hoffa in Detroit
Xaviera Hollander in New York
Carl Jung in Zurich
G. Gordon Liddy in Washington
Alice R. Longworth in Washington
Imelda Marcos in Manila

Groucho Marx in Hollywood
Nostradamus in Paris
Jacqueline Onassis in Washington
George Patton in Frankfurt
F. D. Roosevelt in Campobello
Bertrand Russell in Boston
Gloria Steinem in New York
Margaret Thatcher in London
Duke of Windsor in Paris

PLUTO INCONJUNCT ASC
- many crises occur which are life threatening and highly traumatic
- forced to undergo dramatic and drastic changes in lifestyle
- often driven by compulsive forces
- hard to control basic impulses
- always acts in an extreme manner
- possible manic behavior
- resists all attempts to remake one's character or to alter old ideas or habit patterns
- fights with those who try to guide you into more productive arenas
- overly dominating and bossy
- hates to lose control
- wants to be number one or nothing at all
- one's personality transforms the situation without you even trying
- many psychological changes
- sexual liaisons assume overwhelming importance
- problems relating to others on an equal basis

Bismarck in Berlin
E. B. Browning in Florence
Carol Burnett in Hollywood
Enrico Caruso in New York
F. S. Fitzgerald in Hollywood
Greta Garbo in Hollywood
Jean Genet in Paris
Alfred Hitchcock in Hollywood
Henry Kissinger in Washington
John Lennon in New York
Margaret Mead in Samoa
Paul Newman in Hollywood
Yoko Ono in New York
Aristotle Onassis in Buenos Aires
Mary Pickford in Hollywood

Mme de Pompadour in Paris
R. L. Stevenson in Samoa
Woodrow Wilson in Washington and Paris

PLUTO OPPOSITE ASC/CONJ DESC
- intense interaction with the public manifests changes in overall outlook
- others have to try twice as hard to reach you
- keeps others at a distance
- refuses to compromise or give up control
- loves a good fight or debate
- often manipulative and intolerant
- feelings blow alternately hot and cold
- frequent love-hate relationships
- enemies become friends and vice versa
- must be completely honest and fair
- often tries to remake or remold the partner
- puts others under a microscope
- sheer penetrating insight with x-ray vision
- very combative, competitive and highly sexed
- uses one's body as a bargaining tool
- hostile attitude towards the world causes danger and violence eruptions
- often feels desperate, lonely or abandoned
- insatiable thirst for power, control and authority

Helen G. Brown in New York
Catherine the Great in Leningrad
Enrico Fermi in Chicago
Sigmund Freud in Vienna
Clark Gable in Hollywood
Nikolai Lenin in Moscow
Charles Lindbergh in New York
Manuel Noriega in Panama
Gavrilo Princip in Sarajevo
Barbra Streisand in Hollywood
Mark Twain in San Francisco

PLUTO CONJUNCT MC
- makes an impact on the world that few can dare to ignore
- wants to be a person of significance
- thirsts for power and authority
- often oversteps limits and falls victim to scandal or an assassin
- overly possessive and domineering
- many fights with those in authority

- secretive and subtle on one hand yet ruthless and steamrolling on the other
- always seeks to remodel or transform
- good for trouble-shooters or private eyes
- gains fame or notoriety
- has great influence on the public
- could fall victim to corruption
- may use occult means to gain control
- has to be number one
- either worshipped or detested
- others are secretly envious or jealous
- over exalted opinion of self
- could be a dictator or petty tyrant
- highly individualistic
- obsessive and irresistible
- has charisma plus

Catherine de Medici in Paris
James Dean in Hollywood
Charlton Heston in Hollywood
J. F. Kennedy in Dallas
Vivien Leigh in Hollywood
Francois Mitterand in Paris
Lord Mountbatten in New Delhi
William Penn in Philadelphia
Richard I in Jerusalem
Anwar Sadat in Cairo
Franz Schubert in Vienna
Joseph Smith in Nauvoo
Elizabeth Taylor in Rome
Pierre Trudeau in Ottawa
Ken Uston in Las Vegas

PLUTO SEXTILE MC
- abundant talents and expressive personality furthers ambition
- loves getting to the bottom of things
- a natural reporter or investigator
- loves puzzles and enigmas
- interested in psychology or the occult
- wants to save others from disaster
- great ability to sway public opinion
- transforms everyone who comes within reach
- gains support, admiration, cooperation and respect from those in power
- gets those in superior positions to do your bidding

- highly manipulative and mildly coercive
- great organizing ability
- enterprising, visionary and revolutionary

Prince Albert in London
Queen Anne in London
Anita Bryant in Miami
Barbara Bush in Washington
Enrico Caruso in New York
Mary Cassatt in Paris
Frederic Chopin in Paris
Bette Davis in Hollywood
Christian Dior in Paris
Rajiv Gandhi in New Delhi
General Gordon in the Sudan
Hugh Hefner in Hollywood
Ernest Hemingway in Paris
Adolf Hitler in Berlin
Don Johnson in Miami
Michael Landon in Hollywood
Nelson Mandela in Johannesburg
Shirley MacLaine in Hollywood
Joe Montana in San Francisco
Roman Polanski in Hollywood
Elvis Presley in Memphis
Albert Schweitzer in Gabon
Shah of Iran in Teheran
R. L. Stevenson in Samoa
Johann Strauss in Vienna
Shirley Temple in Hollywood
Richard Wagner in Zurich
Joseph Wambaugh in Los Angeles
Woodrow Wilson in Washington

PLUTO SQUARE MC
- wants complete control and desires total autonomy
- won't let anyone take advantage of you
- always has a better way to do things
- very ambitious with a power complex
- oblivious to public opinion or disapproval
- loves money for its own sake
- not above buying someone to further one's goals
- loves to alter the status quo
- good for engineers, urban planners or real estate developers
- a born investigator with keen insight

- knows where the bodies are buried
- some methods incur disfavor with those in authority
- possibility of arrest, imprisonment or even assassination
- one'personality alters the course of history some times for the better
- often antisocial, licentious or over sexed
- abuses positions of power or control
- possibility of financial ruin
- many personal crises
- loves danger and constantly puts oneself in peril

Gloria Allred in Los Angeles
Roseanne Barr in Hollywood
Clara Barton in Washington
Johannes Brahms in Vienna
Lenny Bruce in New York
Richard Burton in Hollywood
Elizabeth I in London
Jackie Gleason in Miami
Che Guevara in Havana
Jesse Helms in Washington
Herbert Hoover in Washington
Janis Joplin in San Francisco
J.F. Kennedy in London
Liberace in Las Vegas
Abraham Lincoln in Washington
Louis XIV in Paris
Douglas MacArthur in Tokyo
Ferdinand Marcos in Manila
Mata Hari in Paris
Josef Mengele in Auschwitz
Harvey Milk in San Francisco
Rupert Murdoch in London
Ronald Reagan in Washington
William Rehnquist in Washington
Gloria Swanson in Hollywood
Harry Truman in Tokyo
Tina Turner in Dallas

- strong need to succeed
- great ambition
- seldom uses underhanded or sneaky means to attain control
- understands power and doesn't abuse it when it's offered
- approaches others with penetrating insight
- high degree of intuition
- usually gets what one wants with little effort
- great measure of influence
- very magnetic and compelling
- often irresistible, magnetic and compelling
- your very presence alters the perceptions of those with whom you come in contact

Lucille Ball in Hollywood
Helena Blavatsky in New York
Christopher Boyce in Mexico City
E. B. Browning in Florence
Al Capone in Chicago
Fidel Castro in Havana
Prince Charles in London
Van Cliburn in Moscow
Father Damien in Hawaii
J. P. Getty in London
William Gladstone in London
Francisco Goya in Madrid
Hirohito in Tokyo
John Holmes in Hollywood
Jim Jones in Guyana
Rudyard Kipling in London
Madonna in Hollywood
Bette Midler in New York
Napoleon III in Paris
Louis Pasteur in Paris
H. Ross Perot in Dallas
Eleanor Roosevelt in Washington
Lowell Thomas in Lhasa
Robert Urich in Las Vegas
Rudolph Valentino in Hollywood

PLUTO TRINE MC
- years for complete power and control the environment
- highly possessive
- life is cluttered with nonessentials
- compulsive and self absorbed

PLUTO INCONJUNCT MC
- resents others having control over your life
- many power struggles
- resists any attempt to remake or manipulate one's thoughts or actions
- many confrontations with those in authority

- others must give you a loose rein
- highly destructive at times
- often lays waste to everything in sight
- has a violent temper
- very passionate and intense
- must learn moderation and self control
- attracts those who often use you for their own selfish gain
- secretive and sneaky
- seldom lays one's cards on the table
- knows where the bodies are buried
- could be a detective or a reporter
- has problems with letting go of the past
- sexuality is often a problem or major issue in close contacts

Konrad Adenauer in Bonn
Fatty Arbuckle in Hollywood
Truman Capote in New York
Coco Chanel in Paris
Henry Ford II in Detroit
Frederick the Great in Berlin
Zsa Zsa Gabor in Hollywood
Jean Genet in Paris
Henry VIII in London
Hindenburg in Berlin
Victor Hugo in Paris
D. H. Lawrence in Taos
David Lloyd George in London
Peter Max in New York
Mies van der Rohe in Chicago
Napoleon I on St. Helena
Eva Peron in Buenos Aires
Leontyne Price in New York
Cecil Rhodes in Rhodesia
Carroll Righter in Hollywood
Norman Schwarzkopf in Kuwait
Joseph Stalin in Moscow
Orson Welles in Hollywood
Yogananda in Los Angeles

- parental types try to control and manipulate your every move
- considerable trauma makes one fearful and paranoid about one's surroundings
- possibility of giving birth to a new personality or identity
- could alter one's name
- personal life goes through much strife, turmoil, upheaval and suffering
- must come to terms with one's own mortality
- should strive for a spiritual outlook
- frequent brushes with danger places your life in jeopardy
- must abandon all desire for power and control
- seeks to elevate oneself
- could serve as a role model for others
- your name is always remembered here in this location

Martin Bormann in Berlin
Sir Richard Burton in Mecca
Gerald Ford in San Francisco
W. G. Harding in San Francisco
L. B. Johnson in Vietnam
Carl Jung in Zurich
R. F. Kennedy in Washington
Martin Luther King in Memphis
Pat Nixon in Washington
Erwin Rommel at El Alamein
Rod Serling in Hollywood
Steven Spielberg in Hollywood
Mother Teresa in Calcutta
Tokyo Rose in Tokyo
Boris Yeltsin in Moscow

PLUTO OPPOSITE MC/CONJ IC
- compulsive and obsessive about security, privacy and security
- bad habits are difficult if not impossible to break
- highly opinionated
- may be considered very biased or prejudiced

SECTION III

THE LOCAL SPACE CHART

What part of a region is best for success and happiness? What part of a metropolitan area will be best to live in and in what part of town should I seek employment? Which areas might be dangerous and threaten my ability to make good judgments? Until the emergence of local space charts, the above questions were unable to be answered, except in the most general of terms.

Calculating your local space chart is relatively easy, providing you have a rudimentary knowledge of geography or mathematics. Your horoscope is an exact opposite of a roadmap. When you look at a birthchart, the top of the horoscope is south, the bottom of the chart is north. The Ascendant is east while the Descendant is west. In other words, the Sun rises over your left shoulder and sets over your right. A roadmap is 180 degrees opposite: east is on the right side of the map while north is at the top, and so on around the map.

With this anomaly in mind, take a piece of paper, fold it in two from top to bottom and draw a faint line down the middle. Then get out a plastic wheel with degree segments from 0 to 360 along the outside of the wheel. Zero will always be due north, 90 degrees means due east, 180 degrees equals south while 270 equals west, just like the navigational instruments used by pilots and ship captains. From the zero point which equals the Midheaven of your natal or relocated chart, calculate the number of degrees each planet is from that zero point.

For example, if you have a planet in the twelfth house of your relocated chart just above the ASC, then it will appear on the right side of the local space map. If you have a planet conjunct your relocated IC or fourth house cusp, then it will appear at the top of the local space map. If you would prefer, you can have a computer firm such as ACS in San Diego do the calculations for you.

Place the center of the plastic wheel or compass at city hall of the city you're investigating. In order to do this, you'll first have to go out and get a detailed map of the community before you can progress further. The reason for putting the center of the wheel on city hall is because that edifice is the administrative and political heart of the city or town, thus the center of activity per se.

Liberace's local space chart for Las Vegas is computed as follows:

Planet	Distance from the IC
Uranus	2 degrees
Moon	105 degrees
Saturn	222 degrees
Neptune	237 degrees
Jupiter	260 degrees
Pluto	268 degrees
Venus	268 degrees
Sun	308 degrees
Mars	310 degrees
Mercury	332 degrees

Placing the center of the wheel at City Hall in Las Vegas, we note that only one planet falls into the sector which corresponds to the Las Vegas Strip, also known as Las Vegas Blvd. which runs parallel to I-15. That planet is Saturn, ruler of Liberace's natal ASC and ruler of the relocated chart's second house of income and assets. The position of Saturn in this type of chart is often indicative of heavy responsibilities and if found in that part of town where you're forced to buckle down and submit to authority. I've found that each planet has a corresponding vibration in the opposite direction as well. In Liberace's local space chart, that opposition falls close to his Uranus line, ruler of his natal second house. From these placements, one quickly sees that the Las Vegas Strip area is good for Liberace where money is concerned.

For those just arriving into a specific community for the first time, using the local space chart often tells them at a glance which areas of town they should investigate, and which parts of town they should steer clear of. If you're already living in a town to which you relocated sometime ago, then place the center of the plastic wheel over your place of residence as you've already made up your mind where to hang your hat. For some strange reason, I've always lived in the part of town which corresponds to my Neptune line. At first this seemed unusual until I remember that Neptune sits in my natal fourth house. Insert your ASC into the local space chart which will fall anywhere from 45 degrees to 135 degrees from the IC if you were born in North America. Unless your relocated chart has the MC exactly square the MC/IC axis, your ASC will fall either side of the 90-degree line on the wheel.

You may also wish to place the plastic wheel onto a map of the USA or any other continent you're curious about. The center of the wheel should be over your birthplace. Note in which direction your planets fall. In my chart, for example, I have Saturn and Uranus east northeast of my birthplace, so any community on the East Coast would respond to those vibrations. My Jupiter line is 32 degrees from my IC, so a locale northeast of my birthplace would bring out the positive nature of Jupiter. The opposite also holds true due to the opposite pole of Jupiter: places southwest of my birthplace would also be favorable, and that is California for me, one of the reasons I feel quite at home in this state. To ascertain exactly which cities around the world intersect your planetary lines, you'll have to seek the services of ACS in San Diego or some other computer firm which can draw that kind of map for you.

MEANING OF THE PLANETARY LINES IN THE LOCAL SPACE CHART

SUN lines refer to that part of town where our creative juices flow much easier. Good for romance, amusements and speculation. Here we're appreciated for being ourselves and where our individuality shines.

MOON lines show where we feel most at home, or where we would like to spend more time. This is the ideal sector for residence and where you take an interest in community affairs. Good for real estate and bargain shopping as well.

MERCURY lines show where we should go to find work. All commercial ventures seem to prosper here and people take note of you. This is also a good area for study and attending lectures or seminars.

VENUS lines show where pleasure may be found and where romance is the most available. You perceive a beauty about this part of town that many might overlook, but hold onto your wallet as you're also likely to spend more in this area than is prudent. Good area for social occasions or earning money.

MARS lines go through that part of town where we expend considerable energy, either in sporting events or provoking conflict. This part of town is stressful and full of tension, so watch out for accidents or injuries. Sexual activity is likely to be intense and quite frequently sought.

JUPITER lines show where we're able to express ourselves, especially to those of different cultures or ethnic backgrounds. Extremely beneficial on either the materialistic or philosophical level, here we can be free to explore the beauties of nature while hiking through the woods or in quiet meditation. This area is likely to be expensive, however, so watch your budget.

SATURN lines are often the most depressing due to burdens placed on us in this part of town. Sometimes we're drawn here because it represents reality, stability and permanence. Providing you're willing to work hard, this is a good area to find work, but you'll have to put up with delays and obstructions along the way. Generally not the most genial or convivial part of town, here life is serious and goal-oriented.

URANUS lines show where you can expect sudden and unexpected situations to develop. Stimulating and exciting, this isn't the part of town in which to relax as your nerves are constantly on edge. Watch out for accidents or risky ventures. Not the best area for stability, but if you're looking to have your battery recharged, this is the area to explore.

NEPTUNE lines show where we may attain peace and serenity, that region where we can escape from the pressures of everyday life. Beauty and harmony are perceived on an ethereal level here and romance takes on an erotic overtone. Watch out for those people who could involve you in drugs or other illegal activities. Control your intake of alcohol in this area as your sensitivity to outside stimuli and resistance to negative forces are at their nadir.

PLUTO lines show that part of town where potential danger lurks in the shadows. You could be placed into life-threatening situations and by the time you call the cops, it's too late. Not the best part of town for peace of mind as you're under constant pressure either from yourself or others. Sex is quite intense and cathartic but with the ever-present aura of violence or coercion. Unless you're involved in the underworld or seek to learn things you may later regret, one should generally stay out of this part of town as it's too intimidating for most people.

Most places are limited by their geography. River cities and seaports don't often spread out in all directions like cities in the middle of a country. If you have most of your planets on the western side of your natal or relocated chart, then you would initially be limited in places like Memphis or Seattle, unless you remember about the polarity of the planets in the local space chart. If most of your planets are in the eastern sector of your chart, then places like Milwaukee or Detroit might present the same problem unless you remember polarity.

If more than one individual is involved when relocating, and no single area appears to be the best for all concerned, it might be wise to choose an area where no lines are present. This then becomes a neutral area where no one particular individual asserts their personality to such a degree that cooperation becomes totally impossible.

SECTION IV

THE GEODETIC CHART

The geodetic chart operates on the premise that it is possible to predict how an individual will fit into the general scheme of things in a particular locale. Being extremely impersonal, the geodetic chart will show how the environment affect the individual and major events which might occur in a specific region, such as hurricanes, tornadoes, earthquakes, etc. The symbolism of this type of chart is more fated than is the interpretation of the natal chart for there's no free will and you're at the mercy of the elements.

There are many types of geodetic charts from which to choose. The oldest to my knowledge is the one developed and popularized by Sepharial during the 19th century whereby the Greenwich meridian (0 degrees) became 0 Aries and the world neatly apportioned in 30 degree segments working eastward. Thus a locale at 151 degrees east, like Sydney Australia, was given a permanent MC of 1 Virgo. This system was quite simple but relied on your willingness to recognize the Greenwich meridian as the logical point from which to decipher the destiny of the planet we live on. When the Greenwich Observatory was founded in 1675, the British were lords of the high seas, supreme commanders of the oceans with the largest naval force in the world. To me, the Greenwich meridian represents a convenient dividing line, politically motivated, and not one which relates to the natural division of the earth's land masses.

After reading a book on the Great Pyramid of Egypt some years ago, I was astounded to find that it was erected at the center of the world's land mass. Exactly one-fourth of the land lay northeast, one-fourth to the southeast, etc. How the ancients were able to ascertain this with such precision is anyone's guess. But the fact remains, the Great Pyramid meridian relates to the geographical structure of the earth and was never politically motivated. The longitude of the Great Pyramid is 31E09, its latitude being 29N59. This is the only point on this planet

where one can divide the land masses. Thus the use of a geodetic chart which takes this into account must have some significance with respect to geology or meteorology.

The premise of any geodetic system is that each place on this planet has a fixed, and permanent, ASC and MC. Weather predictions made by looking at a geodetic chart are often quite accurate and amazing, especially with respect to earthquakes. The word geodetic is composed of the Greek word "geo" which means earth and "desy" which relates to the mathematics of curved surfaces. Geo is the root word for geography and geology as well. Anything which relates to the world should be relatively fixed in theory, even though with the discovery of plate tectonics, we now know the earth does move a slight degree over billions of years. When you look at a geodetic chart, you're letting the world run the show and you'll have little affect on its overall activity.

A third type of geodetic chart was developed by L.E. Johndro, the eminent Canadian astrologer, born on the same day as Franklin D. Roosevelt. He used the right ascension of a natal or progressed Sun combined with a precessional factor plus or minus the locale of where the specific activity took place. He reasoned that the 0 point of Aries had moved westward 29 degrees 10 minutes from Greenwich in March 1930 which is considerably more than the generally accepted 23-24 degrees used by most sidereal astrologers. He never satisfactorily explained to me why he used this precession until I started investigating the Great Pyramid. Using his precession, we entered the Age of Aquarius in 1990. It takes approximately 72 years for the Sun to move backwards one degree on the ecliptic for a grand total of 25,920 years to complete one circle of the twelve signs of the zodiac. The distance between his precession of 29 degrees 10 minutes and the Great Pyramid of Egypt (which is 31E09) is 60 degrees 19 minutes as of March 1930. Computed to time, this equates to a timespan of about 4344 years. Subtracting that figure from 1930 gives us the date of 2415BC about the time many feel the Great Pyramid was either begun or completed. I do feel that this date somehow represents the date when zero degree of Aries stood over the Great Pyramid; hence like so many other facets of the Pyramid, its position again serves as a mathematical marker in the history of the world and the cosmos.

For this reason, I strongly support using the geodetic system which uses the Great Pyramid of Egypt as the baseline. If you wish to investigate Johndro's system or Sepharial's system, please feel free to do so. I think all of them have something to offer, some more so than others.

The best location is one in which an individual maximizes their strong points and minimizes their deficiencies. It's the place where you hold the trump card, but some horoscopes are so difficult due to their number of "hard" aspects that it's almost impossible to find a place where the individual might find success and good fortune. For some strange reason, that may be the karma with which they were saddled in this lifetime, who knows? Most humans are antennas, picking up and generating signals at will and few of us pay attention to the hidden and obscure vibrations that surround us every moment of the day. But if we sit back and listen to that "inner voice," something might be relayed to us of great value. Most people don't use their progressions as fully as they could to understand how they are moving from one phase of existence into another. Most of us are too wrapped up in keeping our heads above water in the daily struggle for survival. We tend to rely or depend on vibrations coming in from the outside world (transits) in order to plan our existence. To me this is letting someone or something control my destiny. By knowing how we fit into the grand scheme of things from the geodetic chart, we are less at the hands of fate and may anticipate events or circumstances that may alter our perspective on life.

Putting it another way, most people are batteries. There are some places where our energy fields continually operate at peak efficiency and other places require us to get frequent jump starts. Your battery isn't really dead, just in need of assistance. We all attract and repel certain forces, or people, regardless of our location. Some places seem to be more positively charged for us than others and the geodetic chart shows where you won't need those daily recharges just to get on top of things. No place on earth is completely positive, however, for life is a series of compromises we make each day in order to function. Some places on this planet are more attuned to our particular and unique personality and it's the aim of the astrologer or reader to locate that spot where our vibrations receive the least static and where our "radio set" may operate at peak efficiency and get the largest audience.

We're now going to look at the pyramid charts for the five people already mentioned who made it big in Las Vegas. The fixed, or permanent, MC is 3 Scorpio 42, the ASC is 12 Capricorn 28. For your amusement or curiosity, I've included Las Vegas' natal planets into its geodetic wheel, but for the purposes of this section, I suggest you place your own planets there instead.

Las Vegas, Nevada
May 15, 1905

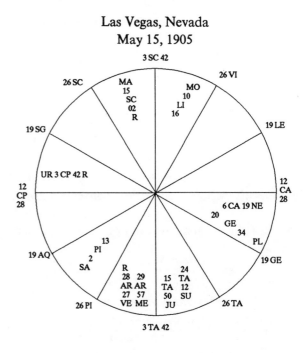

Figure 11. Geodetic Chart for Las Vegas.

Placing Howard Hughes' planets into the fixed wheel is quite revealing. Note the conjunction of the Sun and Uranus in the twelfth house of secrets

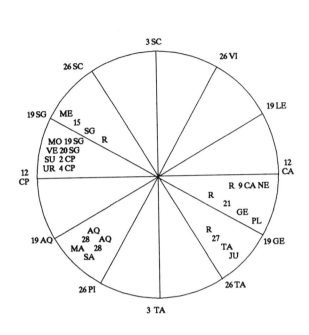

Figure 12. Geodetic Chart for Howard Hughes.

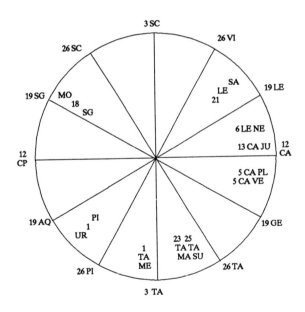

Figure 13. Geodetic Chart for Liberace.

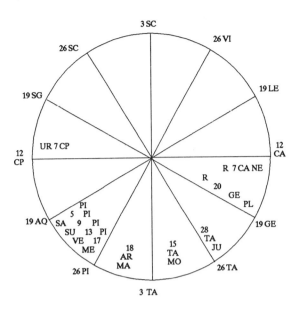

Figure 14. Geodetic Chart for Bugsy Siegel.

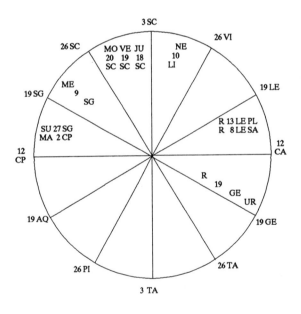

Figure 15. Geodetic Chart for Robert Urich.

and quest for privacy. The Moon and Venus, rulers of the geodetic IC and DESC, are there as well. This would not be a good place for this particular individual to lead a prominent social life. Mars and Saturn in the second house of acquisitions is borne by history, especially when you note they're both square Jupiter in the fifth house of speculation. Most of the planets are on the eastern side of the chart so Hughes wouldn't have to wait around for others to activate his battery.

Liberace's natal MC and the geodetic MC for Las Vegas are almost identical, and the ASC is Capricorn to boot. When this occurs, an individual really feels they have something in common with that place and that success and fortune probably come with ease.

The two entities seem to act with little conflict of interest and the relationship is mutually satisfying. The chief difference is that Venus and Pluto, rulers of Liberace's natal MC and IC, are now trine the MC instead of being in opposition to his natal ASC. Jupiter is opposite the ASC, a clear indication of his fame and wealth in that city.

Bugsy Siegel's geodetic placements offer considerable illumination as to his overall effect on this gambling mecca. Four planets in the second house, including the ruler of the geodetic ASC trining the MC, made Siegel a major force in this town. But the ruler of the geodetic MC is sesquare the MC which created numerous problems for him while trying to accomplish his mission. Pluto sits in the sixth house which rules unions and the work force in general, and Pluto often acts in rather underhanded ways. Siegel's Moon trines the ASC, and as ruler of the geodetic DESC, probably made him numerous enemies which precipitated his early demise the year following the opening of his resort hotel.

We find ambivalence in Robert Urich's geodetic chart for Las Vegas. Mars, natally in his fifth house, sextiles the geodetic MC but is placed in the twelfth house of sorrow and sadness. Pluto, ruler of the geodetic MC, inconjuncts the ASC yet the

Moon and Venus, rulers of the geodetic IC and DESC are conjunct in the tenth house. Neptune squares the ASC/DESC axis clearly illustrating the frustration and feeling of alienation Urich felt in this plastic oasis. Neptune also rules impermanence and artificiality and he felt those characteristics shouldn't be present where children were concerned.

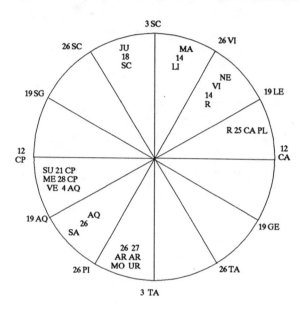

Figure 16. Geodetic Chart for Ken Uston.

In Ken Uston's case, Venus, ruler of his natal DESC, squares the geodetic MC along with Mars, co-ruler of his natal ASC and ruler of his natal sixth house of work and employment. Since Venus and Mars are rulers of his ASC/DESC axis, problems would no doubt result relating to his reputation or professional status and would conflict with his desire for security and peace of mind. Las Vegas could be quite dangerous for Uston in the long run unless he learned to play it cool. Neptune, ruler of his natal IC, trines the geodetic ASC, so Uston felt quite at home in this town despite the numerous difficulties he encountered. Saturn in the second inconjunct the ruler of the geodetic MC in the seventh shows why he was barred from the casinos, thus cutting off his source of income and reason for being there in the first place.

The geodetic chart by nature indicates gravity, being grounded to a place by something you can neither control nor comprehend. Forces are at work which you cannot see and conditions present which require you to "go with the flow" or suffer the consequences. You cannot read a geodetic chart on a psychological level for that implies a certain level of free will which this type of chart does not allow. Thousands of people are born on the same day, and to presume they would all relate to a specific place in the same manner is stretching credibility to the limit. You'll always have to return to the natal chart if you have an accurate birthtime, and see which planets rule the natal angles and then see where they fall into the geodetic chart. Note where the rulers of the geodetic angles fall in your chart and you should have a pretty good idea of how you're going to relate to this environment. This type of chart has its limitations, but the geodetic chart should always be analyzed before recommending a suitable spot for relocation.

GEODETIC COORDINATES USING THE GREAT PYRAMID SYSTEM

The following table lists the Midheavens for major cities around the world according to the Great Pyramid of Egypt as the baseline or prime meridian. If you prefer using the Sepharial system, simply add 31°09'.

UNITED STATES OF AMERICA

City	Coord	City	Coord
Birmingham, AL	2SA03	Duluth, MN	26SC44
Anchorage, AK	28VI57	Minneapolis, MN	25SC35
Little Rock, AR	26SC34	Jackson, MS	29SC39
Phoenix, AZ	6SC47	Kansas City, MO	24SC16
Los Angeles, CA	0SC36	St. Louis, MO	28SC39
San Diego, CA	1SC42	Billings, MT	10SC21
San Francisco, CA	26LI26	Omaha, NB	22SC50
Denver, CO	13SC52	Las Vegas, NV	3SC42
Hartford, CT	16SA10	Reno, NV	29LI03
Wilmington, DE	13SA18	Manchester, NH	17SA23
Washington, DC	11SA50	Atlantic City, NJ	14SA24
Jacksonville, FL	7SA12	Newark, NJ	14SA41
Miami, FL	8SA40	Albuquerque, NM	12SC12
Tampa, FL	6SA24	Buffalo, NY	9SA58
Atlanta, GA	4SA28	New York, NY	14SA54
Savannah, GA	7SA45	Charlotte, NC	8SA00
Honolulu, HI	20VI59	Fargo, ND	22SC03
Boise, ID	2SC38	Cincinnati, OH	4SA20
Chicago, IL	1SA12	Cleveland, OH	7SA09
Indianapolis, IN	2SA42	Columbus, OH	5SA51
Des Moines, IA	25SC14	Oklahoma City, OK	21SC21
Wichita, KS	21SC31	Tulsa, OK	22SC56
Louisville, KY	3SA05	Portland, OR	26LI14
New Orleans, LA	28SC47	Philadelphia, PA	13SA41
Shreveport, LA	25SC06	Pittsburgh, PA	8SA50
Portland, ME	18SA35	San Juan, PR	22SA44
Baltimore, MD	12SA14	Providence, RI	17SA27
Boston, MA	17SA47	Charleston, SC	8SA55
Detroit, MI	5SA48	Sioux Falls, SD	22SC07

Memphis, TN	28Sc48	Norfolk, VA	12Sa34
Nashville, TN	2Sa04	Richmond, VA	11Sa24
Dallas, TX	22Sc02	Seattle, WA	26Li31
El Paso, TX	12Sc22	Spokane, WA	1Sc27
Houston, TX	23Sc29	Charleston, WV	7Sa13
San Antonio, TX	20Sc21	Milwaukee, WI	0Sa56
Salt Lake City, UT	6Sc58	Cheyenne, WY	14Sc02
Burlington, VT	15Sa39		

CANADA

Calgary, Alta.	4Sc46	Halifax, NS	25Sa15
Edmonton, Alta.	5Sc23	Ottawa, Ont.	13Sa09
Vancouver, BC	25Li44	Toronto, Ont.	9Sa28
Winnipeg, Man.	21Sc42	Montreal, PQ	15Sa17
St. John, NB	22Sa48	Quebec City, PQ	17Sa35
St. John's, Nfld	6Cp08	Regina, Sask.	14Sc12

MEXICO

Acapulco, Gue.	18Sc56	Mexico City, DF	19Sc42
Guadalajara, Jal.	15Sc31	Veracruz, Ver.	22Sc43

LATIN AMERICA

Buenos Aires, Arg.	0Cp24	San Salvador, ES	29Sc39
Nassau, Bahamas	11Sa30	Guatemala City, Gua.	28Sc20
Bridgetown, Bar.	29Sc14	Georgetown, Guyana	0Cp41
Hamilton, Bermuda	24Sc05	Port au Prince, Hai.	16Sa31
La Paz, Bolivia	20Sc42	Tegucigalpa, Hon.	1Sa38
Bahia, Brasil	20Cp20	Kingston, Jamaica	12Sa03
Rio de Janeiro, Br.	15Cp35	Managua, Nicaragua	2Sa34
Sao Paulo, Brasil	12Cp14	Panama City, Panama	9Sa19
Santiago, Chile	18Sa11	Asuncion, Paraguay	1Cp11
Bogota, Colombia	14Sa46	Lima, Peru	11Sa48
San Jose, CR	4Sa46	Port of Spain, Tr.	27Sa20
Havana, Cuba	6Sa29	Montevideo, Uru.	2Cp40
Santo Domingo, DR	18Sa57	Caracas, Venezuela	21Sa55
Quito, Ecuador	10Sa21		

AFRICA

Algiers, Alg.	1Pi54	Dakar, Senegal	11Aq25
Luanda, Angola	12Pi05	Cape Town, SA	17Pi13
Cairo, Egypt	0Ar06	Johannesburg, SA	26Pi51
Addis Ababa, Eth.	7Ar33	Khartoum, Sudan	1Ar23
Accra, Ghana	28Aq38	Dar es Salaam, Tan.	8Ar08
Nairobi, Kenya	5Ar40	Tunis, Tunisia	9Pi02
Tripoli, Libya	12Pi02	Kampala, Uganda	1Ar16
Casablanca, Mor.	21Aq16	Kinshasa, Zaire	14Pi09
Maputo, Mozam.	1Ar16	Lusaka, Zambia	27Pi08

Lagos, Nigeria	2Pi15	Harare, Zimbabwe	0Ar54

AUSTRALIA

Adelaide, SA	17Ca26	Hobart, Tas.	26Ca10
Brisbane, Qld.	1Le53	Melbourne, Vic.	23Ca49
Canberra, ACT	27Ca59	Perth, WA	24Ge41
Darwin, NT	9Ca41	Sydney, NSW	0Le04

NEW ZEALAND AND OCEANIA

Auckland, NZ	23Le37	Suva, Fiji	27Le16
Christchurch, NZ	21Le29	Agana, Guam	23Ca36
Dunedin, NZ	19Le21	Pago Pago, Samoa	8Vi09
Wellington, NZ	23Le38	Papeete, Tahiti	29Vi17

ASIA

Kabul, Afgh.	8Ta03	Amman, Jordan	4Ar47
Dacca, Bang.	29Ta16	Seoul, So.Korea	5Ca49
Rangoon, Burma	8Ge01	Beirut, Lebanon	4Ar21
Peking, China	25Ge16	Kuala Lumpur, Mal.	10Ge33
Shanghai, China	0Ca19	Karachi, Pakistan	5Ta54
Nicosia, Cyprus	2Ar13	Manila, Philippines	29Ge51
Hong Kong/Victoria	23Ge00	Riyadh, S.Arabia	15Ar34
Bombay, India	11Ta41	Singapore	12Ge42
Calcutta, India	27Ta13	Colombo, SriLanka	18Ta42
New Delhi, India	16Ta03	Damascas, Syria	5Ar09
Jakarta, Indo.	15Ge39	Taipei, Taiwan	0Ca21
Teheran, Iran	20Ar17	Bangkok, Thailand	9Ge22
Baghdad, Iraq	13Ar16	Istanbul, Turkey	27Pi49
Jerusalem, Israel	4Ar05	Hanoi, Vietnam	14Ge42
Tokyo, Japan	18Ca36	Saigon, Vietnam	15Ge31

SOVIET UNION

Kiev	29Pi22	Odessa	29Pi35
Leningrad	29Pi06	Vladivostok	10Ca47
Moscow	6Ar26		

EUROPE

Tirana, Albania	18Pi41	Milan, Italy	8Pi03
Vienna, Austria	15Pi11	Palermo, Italy	12Pi13
Brussels, Belg.	3Pi11	Rome, Italy	11Pi20
Sofia, Bulgaria	22Pi10	Venice, Italy	11Pi12
Prague, Czech.	13Pi17	Amsterdam, Neth.	3Pi45
Copenhagen, Den.	11Pi26	Oslo, Norway	9Pi36
London, England	28Aq41	Warsaw, Poland	19Pi51
Helsinki, Fin.	23Pi49	Lisbon, Portugal	19Aq43
Marseille, Fr.	4Pi15	Bucharest, Rum.	24Pi57
Paris, France	1Pi11	Edinburgh, Scot.	25Aq38

Berlin, Germany	12Pi14	Barcelona, Spain	1Pi02
Bonn, Germany	5Pi56	Madrid, Spain	25Aq10
Frankfurt, Germany	7Pi31	Seville, Spain	22Aq52
Munich, Germany	10Pi25	Stockholm, Sw.	16Pi54
Athens, Greece	22Pi34	Geneva, Switz.	5Pi00
Budapest, Hung.	18Pi21	Zurich, Switz.	7Pi23
Reykjavik, Ice.	7Aq00	Belgrade, Yugo.	19Pi21
Dublin, Ireland	22Aq36		

SECTION V

THE DECLINATION CHART

I first discovered how declinations may affect one's destiny in a specific locale shortly before my first book was published in 1972. Not being familiar at the time with other relocation techniques, I was amazed at the ability of this system to pinpoint the environment I had been placed in as well as the types of people I encountered daily. I noted that the declination of Jupiter in my chart was 21N13, exactly half the latitude of Boston. It struck me as more than just mere coincidence, especially since Jupiter rules publishing. I wondered if there was more to this system than met my untrained eye, so when I returned to California I finally found the clue. The missing link was found: one must first multiply the initial declination, then place them on a map of the world, and here's the clincher. One uses the multiplied declination figure not only in latitude, but in longitude as well. I told you this system was weird. There are always two planetary influences operating in any given locale on this planet.

Exactly why this should be eludes me. It's really no more unusual than supposing that two planets which occupy different angles at the same time, called a paran, can have an affect on your life at a specific latitude. Jim Lewis, founder of ASTRO*-CARTO*GRAPHY, uses parans all the time, but since I had never used declinations before, the idea sounded intriguing. I'm a nuts and bolts type of astrologer, not a mathematician, physicist or theoretician. I use what works, and this system works all the time, though I can't tell you the logic or rationale behind it.

Calculating the declination chart is rather difficult, however, unless you send away to a computer firm to get the actual declinations of your planets. Trying to do it yourself might result in an error of one or two minutes and when you get into the higher figures, this could amount to an error of many miles. The room for error is enormous, so don't try to do it yourself.

After you get the right degree of declination, multiply them until you reach 180 degrees, then stop. For those who have planets in late Pisces or Virgo or early Aries or Libra, you'll have to do a lot of multiplications. But for those fortunate individuals who have planets in Cancer and Capricorn, the task won't be nearly as arduous.

Let's use the declinations for Howard Hughes as an example:

Sun	23deg25
Moon	18deg32
Mercury	19deg37
Venus	22deg48
Mars	13deg07
Jupiter	18deg47
Saturn	13deg23
Uranus	23deg38
Neptune	22deg10
Pluto	14deg48
Ascendant	5deg57
Midheaven	22deg30

You'll note I haven't put whether the declination was north or south as it makes no difference in the final analysis.

Let's take Howard Hughes' Moon whose declination is 18°32'. The second multiple of this figure equals 37°04', the third is 55°36', etc. Keep in mind these figures will eventually pertain not only to latitudes north and south of the equator but also to longitudes east and west of Greenwich.

Hughes' Venus declination is 22°48', the second multiple is 45°36', the third is 68°24', etc. Obviously anything above 90 degrees cannot be used for latitudes, only longitudes. Ninety degrees north or south places you at one of the poles.

The next step is to get out a world map, one with lines running east and west as well as north and south giving longitude and latitude. If you can't find one giving those figures, then you'll have to select a specific city, ascertain its longitude and latitude and then see which one of your multiplied declinations falls closest to that point. Pay close attention to which lines intersect and where they intersect. For those not familiar with basic geography, this may be unfamiliar and confusing to say the least. If you were going to see which "declinations" fell through California, jot down on a sheet of paper all declinations from 115 to 125 degrees which corresponds to its longitudes, as well as 32 to 42 degrees, which corresponds to its latitude north and south. Then get out a piece of graph paper and draw the longitude and latitude lines for the area you're investigating.

You may find that a particular metropolitan area falls between two declination lines, depending on how far you go from the center of town. Let's suppose you're in Los Angeles (34N03/118W15) and your Venus declination line sits at 34°00' while your Saturn line sits at 34°10'. Now comes the tricky part: the distance between these two lines is 10 minutes, so divide the difference by two. The dividing line between Venus and Saturn is 34°05'. Now you'll have to get a detailed street map of Los Angeles to ascertain exactly which street corresponds to 34°05'. As it happens, this runs down the middle of Melrose Avenue. Anything south of that street would vibrate to Venus, anything north of that street to Saturn.

On your graph, you should now place the letter "D" in red and next to it the figure 34°05'. Detailed survey maps of most metropolitan areas may be obtained from most map stores or stores which sell government survey material. Assuming the individual who had these Venus and Saturn lines running through Los Angeles had a choice in where to live or work, one could quickly see that they should work in the area corresponding to Saturn and live in the area denoted by Venus.

One also must do the same if multiple lines run north and south through a metropolitan area. Let's say an individual's Sun line (declination multiple) sits at 118°15' and their Mars line sits at 118°25'. The distance between these lines is again 10 minutes, so dividing the difference by two gives 5 minutes of arc, or mileage if you prefer. Looking at an atlas, Los Angeles' longitude at City Hall is 118W15.

Five miles west of this point corresponds to Vine Street in the heart of Hollywood. Anything east of this street falls under the Sun line while locations west of this street vibrate to Mars. The graph for this person's declination lines in Los Angeles would look like this:

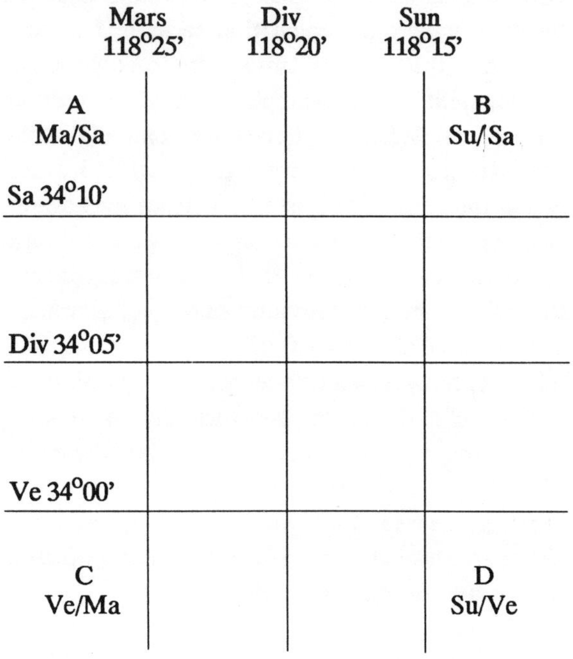

Figure 17. Example Declination Graph
at Los Angeles.

Now comes the second hard part. You'll note that Los Angeles essentially falls into four distinct areas. Two longitude lines and two latitude lines. One thus has the following possibilities: Sun/Venus = Sun/Saturn = Venur/Mars = Mars/Saturn.

Section A relates to Mars/Saturn
Section B relates to Sun/Saturn
Section C relates to Venus/Mars
Section D relates to Sun/Venus

For an individual moving to a city which had these crossings, one might be advised to live and work in either Sections B or D as the harmony one generally seeks would be more forthcoming in those areas of the city. For those venturing into Section A, depression, hard work and delays would be ever present while those traveling into Section A might have to endure violence or physical injury of some kind.

How you interpret the crossings is your individual choice. I prefer to use the Ebertin interpretation as outlined in his book on midpoints. One could also note whether the two planets involved in the crossing were in aspect in the natal chart as well as their house position. For example, I have Venus/Mars crossing in San Francisco. In midpoint analysis, its meaning refers to love, romance and sexual adventure. In my natal chart, both planets are in Scorpio and in the fifth house, thus doubling the previous meaning, even though they're not in aspect to one another. Venus rules my fifth and Mars rules my eleventh. So besides love and romance, friendships and club activity would be important to me in San Francisco. All of the above are true.

One of the greatest assets of the declination chart is the fact you can use it for people who have only an approximate birthtime. With the exception of the Moon's declination, the other nine "planets" will be pretty close to the truth. Like the geodetic systems, you'll get a reasonably accurate portrait of an individuals life in a specific locale. But while the geodetic chart is overwhelmingly environmental in scope, the declination chart appears to concentrate more on the types of people, rather than actual situations, one encounters from place to place.

When you find an area where your ASC and MC lines are prominent, this place will be very important to your development as a person. The best lines seem to be those involving the Sun, Venus and Jupiter. Those involving Mars and Uranus can be problematic, while Saturn, Neptune and Pluto are often catastrophic. If the lines passing through an area are mixed, such as Venus/Saturn, their interpretation must be judged accordingly, just as if those two planets were involved in a single midpoint or were in close aspect in the natal chart.

Sometimes you will run across an area where the two lines involve the same planet, like Sun/Sun for example. That locale bears the full force of that

planet and should be judged by what sign, house and aspects that planet makes in the natal chart.

For example, Ernest Hemingway had a Mars/Mars crossing in Ketchum, Idaho, where he committed suicide with a firearm. Mars (guns) sits natally in his first house square Saturn (depression) in the fourth (end of life) and square Neptune (suicide) and Pluto (death) in the tenth (fame and reputation).

John F. Kennedy had a Neptune/Neptune, or double Neptune, crossing in Washington, D.C. Natal Neptune (visions and dreams) sits in his tenth house conjunct Saturn (responsibility) and sextile the Sun (personal image) in the eighth. Kennedy's ideals inspired an entire generation of young people despite his short term in office. Theodore Roosevelt had a double Sun crossing in Washington, D.C. The Sun conjuncts Mercury in his fifth house opposing Pluto. The fire, energy and vitality which Roosevelt exuded came into full view during his years in the White House where he was known as a "trust buster" by exposing corruption in big business.

Having worked with declinations for nearly two decades, it never ceases to amaze me what the crossings portend. You don't even have to journey to those places to experience their influence. My Sun line, for example, is 16°38', the second multiplication being 33°16'. Any place along this line, north or south of the equator, will have a solar vibration for me. On this latitude are Los Angeles, Phoenix, Dallas and Atlanta in the USA and south of the equator lie Buenos Aires, Cape Town and Sydney. But life is not all one-sided: if you feel positively about a particular place, then people in that area will generally give you positive feedback as well. If the crossing is negative, however, you probably can't wait to leave town and those living there can't wait to see you leave town.

Now we're going to see how these crossings affected some famous people:

AL CAPONE: Sun/Neptune in Chicago and Mars/Pluto in San Francisco. The Sun governs one's individuality, Neptune rules alcohol. Capone was the King (Sun) of booze (Neptune) in Chicago during the Roaring 20's but the government (Sun) got him for tax evasion (Neptune) and sent him to Alcatraz where he was incarcerated (Mars) with hardened criminals (Pluto).

ERNEST HEMINGWAY: Sun/Venus in Havana and Sun/Mars in Madrid. Hemingway was deeply loved and admired (Venus) in Cuba where he lived prior to his rising fame (Sun). Fighting in the Spanish Civil War gave him an outlet for physical activity (Mars).

JOHN F. KENNEDY: Jupiter/Saturn in Boston and Mars/Neptune in Dallas. Kennedy was born into a wealthy family (Jupiter) with strong business and political connections (Saturn). His tenure as President inspired considerable idealism (Neptune) but gained enmity of organized crime. His assassination in Dallas (Mars) was part of a conspiracy (Neptune) which has never been fully revealed.

MARTIN LUTHER KING, JR.: Sun/Venus in Atlanta and Saturn/Neptune in Memphis. King (Sun) came up through the ranks to become the undisputed leader of the civil rights movement. Based from his home in Atlanta, he was greatly loved and admired for his objection to force (Venus) to obtain his goals. He reached a crossroads in Memphis which threatened his authority (Saturn) and was consequently assassinated (Neptune) thus touching off scores of riots in ghettos across our country.

CHARLES LINDBERGH: Sun/Venus in Paris and Mercury/Pluto in New York. Lindbergh became a God (Sun) after his solo flight across the Atlantic. Showered with gifts, honors and titles (Venus), he was the most universally loved person of his time. Soon after his son was kidnapped (Pluto), he was hounded mercilessly by the press (Mercury) who invaded his privacy and peace of mind.

RICHARD NIXON: Venus/Uranus in Washington and Mercury/Venus in Los Angeles. Nixon's term of office was fraught with a warped sense of values

(Venus). Often saying the opposite of what he meant (Uranus), he was forced to resign (Uranus) and moved to California where he had more peace of mind (Venus) and could spend time writing his memoirs (Mercury).

JACQUELINE KENNEDY ONASSIS: Uranus/-Pluto in Washington and Venus/Uranus on the island of Scorpios, Greece. This First Lady created quite a stir when she first arrived in the White House (Uranus) and soon revolutionized the fashion industry (Pluto). She refurbished the White House (Pluto) and riveted the attention of the world during the funeral of her husband (Pluto). She married Onassis quite suddenly (Venus) and their relationship was unconventional, often shocking high society (Uranus).

FRANKLIN D. ROOSEVELT: Mercury/Saturn on Campobello island and Uranus/Pluto in Washington. Roosevelt caught a virus while vacationing on Campobello which later turned into polio, which severely limited (Saturn) his ability to move around (Mercury). It didn't deter him from pursuing a political career which eventually led to the White House. His twelve years in office were a time of trial for the nation (Pluto) and FDR's many programs revolutionized our system of government (Uranus).

LEON TROTSKY: Jupiter/Pluto in Leningrad, Uranus/Uranus in Moscow and Uranus/Pluto in Mexico City. Trotsky was one of the leaders of the Russian Revolution (Jupiter) who might have filled Lenin's shoes had not Stalin barged in and taken the helm (Pluto). After the capital was moved to Moscow, Trotsky was exiled (Uranus) and fled to Mexico City where he was assassinated (Pluto) by Stalinist agents who wanted to forever silence this upstart (Uranus) who some call the "conscience of the Russian revolution."

RUDOLPH VALENTINO: Mercury/Uranus in Hollywood and Mars/Saturn in New York. Valentino was probably the most talked-about (Mercury) actor of his time. Constantly questioned about his masculinity, he gained the admiration of the American woman in ways contrasting to the rustic manners of the American male (Uranus). Shortly after arriving in New York in 1926, he became depressed and ill (Saturn), developed a high fever (Mars) and died of peritonitis.

There are hundreds more examples about which I could tell, but you get the general picture. The crossings in the declination chart work with such amazing accuracy that you would be foolish not to try them when contemplating a possible site for relocation.

Now for consistency, we'll look at the declination crossings for the five examples we've already become acquainted with in this book.

Looking at Howard Hughes' declinations again, we want to find those closest to Las Vegas at 115W09/36N10. Write down which planets fall between 110 and 120 degrees and those that fall between 30 and 40 degrees. Make two columns:

Latitude		Longitude
37deg04	Moon	111deg12
39deg14	Mercury	117deg42
	Venus	114deg00
39deg21	Mars	118deg03
37deg34	Jupiter	112deg42
	Uranus	118deg10
	Neptune	110deg50
	Pluto	119deg44
35deg42	ASC	113deg03
	MC	112deg30

No declinations are given for the Sun or Saturn as none of their multiplied declinations are anywhere near Las Vegas. The closest planetary declination line to Las Vegas is Venus in the longitude column. The other planet closest to Las Vegas in the latitude column is the Moon. Thus Howard Hughes' planetary crossings in Las Vegas are Moon/Venus.

If you want to include the angles, note that the ASC line is actually closer to Las Vegas than is the

Moon. The dividing line between the Moon and ASC is 36°23'. Las Vegas falls south of this, so by

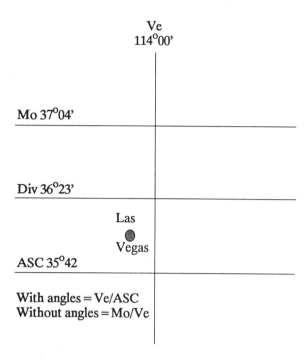

Figure 18. Declination Graph for Howard Hughes.

including the angles, Hughes' crossing in Las Vegas becomes ASC/Venus. Use the ASC and MC declinations only if you have a reasonably accurate birthtime within a few minutes.

Note that the Moon and Venus are in Hughes' natal fourth house, a strong indication of involvement with real estate in this city.

Now we'll do the same for Bugsy Siegel. His original declinations are:

Sun	7°56'	Moon	11°30'
Mercury	6°12'	Venus	7°53
Mars	6°58'	Jupiter	19°18'
Saturn	10°45'	Uranus	23°30'
Neptune	22°17'	Pluto	15°17'
ASC	16°54'	MC	12°22'

Making a list of declination multiples close to Las Vegas, we find:

Latitude		Longitude
39deg40	Sun	119deg00
34deg30	Moon	115deg00
37deg12	Mercury	117deg48
39deg25	Venus	118deg15
34deg50	Mars	118deg26
38deg36	Jupiter	115deg48
32deg15	Saturn	118deg15
	Uranus	117deg30
	Neptune	111deg25
30deg34	Pluto	
33deg48	ASC	118deg18
37deg06	MC	111deg18

Figure 19. Declination Graph for Bugsy Siegel.

Latitude		Longitude
38deg10	the Sun	114deg30
37deg16	Mercury	111deg48
37deg24	Mars	112deg12
	Jupiter	115deg00
31deg10	Saturn	
34deg54	Uranus	116deg20
37deg02	Neptune	111deg06
38deg48	Pluto	116deg24
	ASC	117deg30
36deg15	MC	

Figure 20. Declination Graph for Liberace.

The closest planet to the latitude of Las Vegas is Mercury, the closest in longitude is the Moon. Siegel's crossings in Las Vegas were the Moon/Mercury. If you wish to include the angles, then his crossings become the Moon/MC. Another indication of interest in real estate with possible double dealings as shown by Mercury.

Now, we'll look at Liberace. I won't list the initial declinations as they're shown on his horoscope earlier in this book. The closest lines to Las Vegas are:

Because the Moon and Venus make no crossings near Las Vegas, they're not included on the above list. Liberace's crossings in Vegas are Jupiter/Neptune. If the angles are used, it becomes Jupiter/MC, an excellent indication of the vast fame, good fortune and popularity he achieved in this city

Robert Urich's crossings closest to Las Vegas are Uranus/Neptune. With Bob Urich's Neptune declination at a low degree, nearly everyplace on earth will have a Neptune line running through it. If one uses the angles, then Urich's crossing becomes MC/Uranus, an indication of nervous tension and potential for accidents, as well as general irritability and desire for escape.

Ken Uston's declination lines closest to Las Vegas are Mars/Neptune, one of the worst possible combinations anyone can have. Using the angles, the combination becomes ASC/Mars which is slightly better as Mars rules his natal sixth house of work.

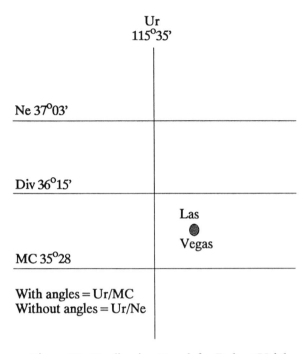

Figure 21. Declination Graph for Robert Urich.

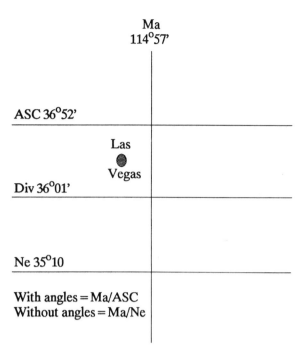

Figure 22. Declination Graph for Ken Uston.

I know the declination system is totally irrational and illogical, but it works! Who ever said the cosmos is orderly? And why this system would work using the Greenwich meridian is anybody's guess, especially since that line was man-made.

By now readers of this book should have calculated their basic relocation chart as well as their geodetic/pyramid charts and the declination graph or map. Some will find that one planet continually keeps cropping up in all charts, while others will find divergence of opinion between the aforementioned charts. In the final analysis, all of them are correct as they're used for different purposes.

Readers who have an accurate birthtime have the knowledge of knowing how much free will is at their disposal by looking at the relocation chart. Those who are sensitive to the environment or climate may find the geodetic chart more illuminating. Those who wish to enlarge their social sphere may find the declination chart has opened up new vistas for them.

There's one more type of chart that may be used when a birthtime is in dispute, and for those who have an accurate birthchart, the next section will of more than average interest.

SECTION VI

PLANETARY LONGITUDES

During my brief stay in Hawaii, I ran across a small pamphlet on relocation entitled *Your Best Place* by D. Warren. Most of the material presented was identical to that outlined in this book with one major exception. The author believed that by adding or subtracting a specific number of degrees from one's natal planets according to the distance of the new place of residence from one's birthplace, startling information could be gleaned not often available from more conventional methods of relocation. If this seems odd or unusual, one does the same basic thing when using solar arc directions by adding the annual motion of the Sun over a number of years onto each planet in the natal chart thus making the solar arc directed Mercury, for example, conjunct natal Venus at a specific time in one's life. In using planetary longitudes, one uses the same premise but places the distance between one planet and another onto a map.

When one erects the conventional relocation chart, one recomputes the MC using the difference in sidereal time from one's birthplace to the place one is erecting the chart for desired residence. In planetary longitudes, one measures the distance in degrees and minutes of longitude the current place of residence is from where the individual was born. For those moving east of their birthplace, one ADDS the difference in longitude degrees and minutes: for those moving west of their birthplace, one SUBTRACTS the difference from each planet in their natal chart.

For example, if you were born in Chicago (87W39) and desired to see what planetary longitudes had in store for you in Los Angeles (118W15), then because Los Angeles is west of Chicago, one subtracts 30°36' from each planet in their chart. If that individual desired to move to Boston (71W04), then that person would add 16°35' onto each planet in his chart. My natal Sun is 15 Scorpio 59: moving west to Los Angeles I would subtract 30°36' from my natal Sun giving me a planetary longitude Sun of 15

Libra 23. If I wanted to see what my planetary longitude Sun was in Boston, I would add 16°35' onto my natal Sun giving me a new Sun position of 2 Sagittarius 34 as Boston is east of Chicago.

The next step is to see whether the new planetary longitude positions aspect a planet in your natal chart, again using only a 3- degree orb. In the case of Los Angeles, my new Sun's position aspects nothing in my natal chart, but in Boston my Sun's position opposes my natal Uranus, sextiles natal Neptune and squares my natal MC. The same number of degrees and minutes may also be added or subtracted from your natal MC, the final figure using this method being only slightly different from that arrived at when computing your relocated chart by the more conventional technique outlined in Section I. The ASC can also be directed forward or backwards, but the planetary longitude ASC will no doubt be quite a bit different than the relocated ASC as computed from the MC of the conventional relocation chart. It works the same way in solar arc directions, so the premise is not all that radical or unusual.

All aspects within 3 degrees should be noted. I've found the most important aspects to be the conjunction and opposition, followed by the square, sextile and trine. All aspects involving Mars, Saturn, Uranus, Neptune and Pluto should be thoroughly analyzed as it can mean the difference between great success or dismal failure.

In my own chart, my brief stay in Hawaii showed my Moon square Saturn, Mercury square the Moon, Venus square Uranus, Saturn opposite Neptune and Jupiter opposite my Sun/Venus conjunction. Needless to say, life there was not all it could have been due to the afflictions to my Moon and that malefic Saturn opposite a planet in my natal fourth house. Here in Los Angeles where I've lived off and on for nearly two decades, my Mercury/Mars conjunction conjuncts Neptune (ruler of my MC) and trines Uranus but Jupiter is within orb to my natal ASC, making life for me considerably more enjoyable in southern California than in any other part of this country.

Now it's time to look at the "new positions" of the planets in the charts of the five examples we've been using throughout this book. Howard Hughes was born in Houston (95W22). As Las Vegas is west of his birthplace, we must SUBTRACT the difference in longitude between Las Vegas and Houston which is 19°47'. from each planet in his natal chart as follows:

Sun	12Sa58	conj. Mercury - opp. MC
Moon	29Sc55	opp. Jup. - sq. Mars/Saturn
Mercury	25Sc15	opp. Jupiter
Venus	0Sa43	-----------
Mars	8Aq24	inconj. Neptune
Jupiter	7Ta56	sex. Neptune
Saturn	8Aq53	inconj. Neptune
Uranus	14Sa30	conj. Mercury - opp. MC
Neptune	19Ge24	conj. Pluto - opp. Moon
Pluto	1Ge44	inconj. Sun/Uranus

From the above positions, we note the Sun/Uranus conjunction hits the IC in Las Vegas, truly indicative of his unusual lifestyle and aloofness in that city. The Moon/Mercury conjunction opposite Jupiter gave him a "larger than life" reputation willing to take risks or gambles speculating in the region. The Mars/Saturn combo inconjunct Neptune made Hughes overly paranoid and apprehensive about his comings and goings while Pluto inconjunct his Sun/Uranus combo sheathed his activities even further in mystery and could have led to his obsessiveness about germs and disease. Jupiter sextile Neptune enlarged his speculative ability and created a vision of Las Vegas unknown since the closing days of World War II.

Liberace was born in West Allis, Wisconsin, (88W-00) and since Las Vegas is west of his birthplace, we must subtract 27°09' from each planet in his natal chart to arrive at the following positions:

Sun	28Ar04	-----------------
Moon	21Sc23	opp. Mars - sq. Saturn
Mercury	4Ar23	sq. Venus/Pluto and ASC
Venus	7Ge54	sex. Neptune
Mars	26Ar16	-----------------
Jupiter	16Ge29	opp. Moon

Saturn	24Ca41	sex. Sun/Mars
Uranus	4Aq23	opp. Neptune - sq. Mercury
Neptune	9Ca37	-----------------
Pluto	8Ge01	sex. Neptune

From the above positions, life was a mixed bag for Liberace in Las Vegas. On one hand, Venus/Pluto sextile Neptune created an aura of glamor and illusion unrivaled in his time or since, but the Moon opposing Mars square Saturn placed heavy demands on his time and energy and also increased his ambition and desire to succeed at all costs. Jupiter opposite the Moon made his life one of excess and abundant extravagance while Saturn sextile his Sun/Mars combo gave him staying power over the years. Mercury square Venus, Pluto and the ASC made him the subject of considerable gossip, especially about his personal life which was finally revealed after his death.

Bugsy Siegel was born in New York (73W57) and since Las Vegas is 41°12' west of his birthplace, this figure is thus subtracted from each planet in his chart.

Sun	28Cp29	trine Jupiter
Moon	4Ar23	sq. Uranus and Neptune
Mercury	5Aq47	inconj. Neptune
Venus	2Aq06	-----------------
Mars	6Pi51	conj. Sun/Sat. - trine Neptune
Jupiter	17Ar40	conj. Mars, sex. Pluto, inc. ASC
Saturn	24Cp45	inconj. MC
Uranus	26Sc30	opp. Jupiter - square MC
Neptune	26Ta30	conj. Jupiter - square MC
Pluto	9Ta31	sex. Sun & Nep. - trine Uranus.

The relocated positions of the Sun, Uranus and Neptune aspecting Jupiter point to Siegel's luck and prominence in this town which he literally put on the map. Moon squaring Uranus and Neptune and Mercury's inconjunct to Neptune indicated numerous frustrations which often threatened to put an end to his dream of a desert gambling mecca. Saturn, Uranus and Neptune adversely aspecting his natal MC gave Siegel energy, persistence and audacity to overcome most of the obstacles and Mars conjunct Sun/Saturn gave him numerous enemies which probably led to his assassination less than a year after his Flamingo Hotel opened for business.

Robert Urich was born in Toronto, Ohio, (80W36) and since Las Vegas is again west of the birthplace, the difference of 34°33' must be subtracted from each natal planet.

Sun	23Sc04	conj. Moon - square ASC
Moon	15Li59	sextile Pluto
Mercury	4Sc50	sextile Mars
Venus	15Li09	sextile Pluto
Mars	27Sc27	square ASC
Jupiter	13Li36	sextile Pluto
Saturn	3Ca33	opposite Mars
Uranus	14Ta53	square Pluto
Neptune	6Vi06	square Mercury
Pluto	8Ca33	square Neptune

No wonder Urich felt so out of place in Las Vegas. Look at the number of aspects to his natal Pluto, ruler of the IC. Pluto is known as the "loner of the zodiac" due to its distance from the center of our solar system. One could hardly feel totally comfortable or secure in such a locale, even if the aspects were relatively favorable. One would literally have to restructure one's lifestyle, something which Urich felt no compunction to do. The Sun/Mars combo adversely aspecting the natal ASC did, however, propel him into our lives during his stint on Vegas but could also have led to his general antipathy for this town which he considered too plastic in which to raise a family.

Ken Uston was born in New York (73W57) and since Las Vegas is 41°12' west of his birthplace, we must subtract that figure from each natal planet.

Sun	10Sa00	-----------------
Moon	15Pi47	trine Jup - opp. Nep - inc. Mars
Mercury	17Sa35	sextile Mars - square Neptune
Venus	23Sa03	sextile Saturn - inconj. Pluto
Mars	3Vi10	conj. MC - inconj. Venus
Jupiter	7Li28	trine Venus
Saturn	14Cp47	trine Neptune - square Mars
Uranus	16Pi19	trine Jup - opp. Nep -inc. Mars
Neptune	3Le12	opp. Venus
Pluto	13Ge51	trine Mars - square Neptune

The Moon/Uranus conjunction trine Jupiter brought Uston luck in this town but their opposition to Neptune created danger and paranoia due to his long winning streak. The reverse seems to be true for Mercury and Pluto aspecting Neptune which favorably aspects Mars. This gave Uston a sense of power and omnipotence, however transient and illusory, to beat the usual odds which always favored the casinos. Jupiter's and Neptune's good aspects to Venus promised big payoffs and a good time but Mars' conjunction to the natal MC created enemies which sought to curb his excessive ambition. In the end it was Saturn's square to Mars which brought his brief reign to an end and exiled him from town once and forever.

After you've relocated your planets in this manner, you will find numerous indications of why life in one particular region or locale progressed in a specific manner. For those contemplating a move to a place they've never been, this system is just as valid as the more conventional technique which subtracts the difference in time from one's birthplace to the desired place of residence or visitation. The big plus for this system, however, is that one doesn't have to have an accurate birthtime in order to use this system, the premise being the same for the geodetic or declination methods already outlined in this book. One should, however, omit the position of the Moon if one is not certain of his moment of birth as it's daily motion is too rapid. The same holds true for the MC and ASC as well.

SECTION VII

CHART COMPARISON OR SYNASTRY

In the past few chapters, we've looked at the basic relocation chart drawn for a specific locale and investigated what that environment has in store from one of the geodetic charts. The main problem with the relocation chart is that it deals only with a metropolitan area, it can't ascertain which community in that region will be compatible with your natal chart. Many people might have Jupiter conjunct their MC along a specific meridian, like 122 west, which runs close to Seattle, Portland, San Francisco and Sacramento. The purpose of this section and the following one on composites, will be to decide which place along a specific planetary line best fits your needs and desires. This is done by comparing your natal horoscope to that of a city, state or country using synastry, which in Greek means "same stars."

Before you begin a chart comparison or synastry, you must first have data from which to compare. There are many official publications, history books and pamphlets which give incorporation dates for cities across America. Few books give the actual founding date; you're lucky to even get the year in most cases. I always try to get the founding date of a place as I feel the incorporation, or charter, date is arbitrary and should not be used unless you happen to be working for the government. My book, *Horoscopes of the Western Hemisphere*, gives the founding dates for over 300 US cities, their birthtimes largely determined by assiduous rectification of events in that city's history. Some consider my work largely speculative, which in a manner it is, but only with respect to the birthtime. The date has been verified by many divergent sources so there is little confusion there. In a manner of speaking, you'll have to trust my judgment and that the charts shown in my book are accurate, which subsequent history seems to have proved beyond a reasonable doubt. But since the birthdate and time for Las Vegas, Nevada, has never been in question, that's the reason I chose it as an example in this book.

The first step in doing a synastry graph is to calculate the aspects between your chart and the city's chart, using only a 3-degree orb. List the aspects on a sheet of paper, dividing it into five columns: conjunctions, sextiles, squares, trines and oppositions. For purposes of synastry, I've eliminated the inconjunct aspect, although you may wish to use it. To decide whether an aspect is positive or negative, remember that sextiles and trines are generally positive, while squares are always negative or problematical. Conjunctions and oppositions can fall into either category depending on the planets involved. Again, aspects involving the Sun, Moon, Mercury, Venus and Jupiter are positive, while those involving Mars, Saturn, Uranus, Neptune and Pluto are negative most of the time. Thus a conjunction of the Sun and Moon is positive while a conjunction involving Mercury and Pluto would be negative. After tallying up the number of positive and negative aspects (and you may use your ASC and MC as well), calculate the number of positive aspects.

Las Vegas, Nevada
May 15, 1905
10:00AM PST

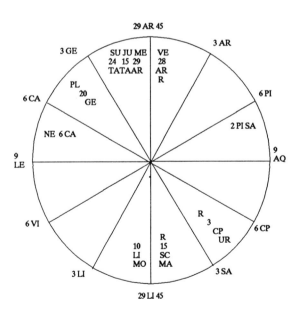

Figure 23. Natal Horoscope of Las Vegas.

Anything less than 60 percent is not advised while anything more than 80 percent could be boring and non-challenging, literally too much of a good thing. I've found that in order for there to be a strong attraction, there should be at least one conjunction in the synastry chart. Obviously if the conjunction involves a "negative" planet, then it could indicate repulsion or difficulty.

When doing a synastry graph, you must now begin to think in terms of multiple entities. Use the words "we and they" in your interpretation which is more impersonal than an analysis between two individuals. Obviously you can't expect to harmonize with everyone in a specific locale, but basic harmony or discordance may be shown with amazing accuracy.

Con.	Sextile	Square	Trine	Opp.
Su-Ur	Su-Sa	Ne-Mo	Su-Me	Mo-Pl
Ur-Ur	Ur-Sa		Su-MC	Ve-Pl
Ju-Su	Asc-Ma		Asc-Ju	
Pl-Pl	Ma-MC			
Ne-Ne	Sa-MC			

Figure 24. Synastry Graph for Howard Hughes and Las Vegas.

Hughes' graph involves 5 conjunctions, only one of them negative. Since Hughes and Las Vegas were born in the same year, their higher octave planets will be conjunct. When this occurs (regardless of whether the planets involved are positive or negative), the conjunction is positive as they're operating on the same wavelength. Hughes' two oppositions are both negative as Pluto in opposition to his Moon and Venus puts severe strain on the emotional and domestic life. A whopping 75 percent of the aspects are positive, showing that Hughes held the cards three times out of four which was clearly shown by his brief stay in this city.

The conjunction of the Sun to Sun and Mercury to Mercury are quite potent. Of the 10 conjunctions, only 40 percent of them are positive. The 8 sextiles and 5 trines are positive while the two squares are negative. Only 3 of the oppositions are positive,

Con.j.	Sextile	Square	Trine	Opp.
Su-Su	Me-Sa	Ju-Mo	Me-Ur	Mo-Pl
Me-Me	Ju-Ju	Sa-Su	Ve-Sa	Ve-Ur
Me-Ve	Sa-Pl		Ju-Ma	Pl-Ur
Me-MC	Ur-Me		Pl-Sa	MC-Me
Ve-Ne	Ur-Ve		MC-Sa	MC-Ve
Ma-Su	Ur-Ur			MC-MC
Ur-Sa	MC-Ur			Asc-Ne
Ne-Asc	Asc-Sa			
Pl-Ne				
Asc-Ur				

Figure 25. Synastry Graph for Liberace and LasVegas.

giving Liberace a total of 32 aspects between his chart and Las Vegas (using a 3-degree orb) for a total of 62.5 percent positive compatibility, within the range of acceptability. This means that Las Vegas gave Liberace positive feedback, and vice versa, at least 62 percent of the time. Holding the cards 5 times out of 8 is better than average and allowed him to perceive change before it was required.

Con.j.	Sextile	Square	Trine	Opp.
Mo-Ju	Me-Ju	Me-Pl	Su-Ne	Mo-Ma
Sa-Sa	Ve-Ju	Ur-Mo	Me-Ma	Ur-Ne
Ne-Ne	Ma-Pl	Ne-Mo	Ve-Ma	Asc-Ju
Pl-Pl	Sa-Ur	MC-Su	Sa-Ne	
Asc-Ma			MC-Me	
			MC-Ve	

Figure 26. Synastry Graph for Bugsy Siegel and LasVegas.

Siegel's conjunctions, like Hughes, involve many similar conjunctions. Four of them are positive while only one opposition is placed on the positive side. Siegel's compatibility with Las Vegas is 68 percent shown by 15 positive aspects and 7 negative ones, well within the acceptable range showing that even adversity had its benefits for Siegel.

Urich's compatibility with Las Vegas is quite good on one hand (66.6 percent positive) due to 16 positive aspects out of 24 all total but harmony is horrible on the other hand. Five conjunctions are present but none of them are positive. When this situation occurs, there's likely to be an aversion or repulsion to a place or person. Only one opposition exists, Jupiter to Jupiter, which is positive and fortunate. Until viewing those negative conjunctions, this would initially appear to be a good place for Urich, but without positive feedback, their relationship is likely to be frustrating, difficult and totally unsatisfactory. From statements made by Urich, this was clearly the case.

Con.j.	Sextile	Square	Trine	Opp.
Ur-Pl	Sa-Mo	Pl-Ju	Su-Me	Ju-Ju
Ne-Mo	Pl-Mo	Pl-Ma	Su-Ve	
Ju-Ma	Me-Mo	Asc-Su	Su-MC	
Ma-Ur	Ma-Sa		Me-Asc	
Sa-Asc	Ne-Asc		Ma-Me	
			Ma-Ve	
			Ma-MC	
			Asc-Me	
			Asc-Ve	
			Asc-MC	

Figure 27. Synastry Graph for Robert Urich and Las Vegas.

Uston's synastry graph reveals 7 conjunctions (four of them negative) and 3 oppositions (only 1 of them negative). The positive aspects number 14 out of a total of 24 giving an overall compatibility of only 58 percent, slightly below what I consider to be an acceptable level. This no doubt led to the problems he encountered in Las Vegas and why he was kicked out of town and told never to return, at least not to the casinos.

In my professional opinion, there should always be some kind of contact between your Sun, Moon and ASC to one of those three points in the city's chart. Any aspect at all is better than none. It doesn't hurt to have an aspect to the city's MC either, especially if you're planning to go into business. For example, I've always been attracted to Portland, Oregon, and when I found it had its Sun in Scorpio conjunct my Moon and its Moon on my ASC, I knew this place

might figure prominently in my life. Besides, the degree on its ASC trines the co-rulers of my tenth house (Uranus and Neptune) and its Jupiter trines my MC.

Con.j.	Sextile	Square	Trine	Opp.
Ju-Ma	Pl-Su	Pl-Ve	Ne-Ju	Ju-Ju
Mo-Me	Ne-Ma	Sa-Su	Su-Su	MC-Sa
Mo-Ve	Sa-Me	Me-Me	MC-Ur	Asc-Su
Mo-MC	Sa-Ve	Me-Ve		
Ur-Me	Sa-MC	ME-MC		
Ur-Ve	MC-Ne			
Ur-MC				

Figure 28. Synastry Graph for Ken Uston and Las Vegas.

Other cities I've lived in have strong similarities as well. Chicago's Sun and Moon conjunct my IC and despite the troublesome times during my youth, I still have great affection for that city. In Boston, where I was first published, my Sun and Venus conjunct its ASC and in San Francisco, its Moon sits right on my Sun/Moon midpoint and its MC is the same degree as my ASC.

You might also wish to insert your planets around the chart of the city you're investigating to determine the general course of your life in that locale. Planets in angular houses should be noted as they precipitate action. Planets in succeedent houses usually grant stability and purpose while those in cadent houses might keep you in the background most of the time.

In Chicago, my Scorpio stellium falls into the twelfth house where it buried my individuality and often placed my life in jeopardy. In San Francisco, my stellium fell into the second house making me quite aware of the high cost of food and rent in that city. In Los Angeles, that stellium falls into the first house creating an entirely different lifestyle and outlook on life, which is probably why I always return to this city after moving to other locales where the pastures momentarily appear to be greener.

The house position of the Sun indicates where you can express your individuality and where you expect to shine. The Moon indicates where you experience fluctuation and change, while Mercury shows where you can parlay your talents in a commercial sense. Venus shows where values may be enlarged or enhanced and where social interaction is to be expected, while Mars indicates where we get "ticked off" and how we expend our excess energy. Jupiter shows where we are most fortunate and sometimes spend or indulge to excess, while Saturn indicates our weak point and where we need to strengthen our defenses. Uranus shows where we can expect surprises and sudden developments, while Neptune indicates where the rug may be pulled out from under us due to confusion, deception or ignorance. Pluto shows where we must reorganize our life and situations that could place us in jeopardy, not to mention certain elements we often prefer to avoid. Pluto always forces us to face an issue head-on, it's either your nemesis or salvation, depending on your viewpoint.

Now that we've ascertained the initial degree of compatibility or disharmony between us and another political entity, it's time to find out whether our individual personalities which appear to be in sync will meld or clash in the long run by analyzing the composite chart.

SECTION VIII

THE COMPOSITE CHART

A composite chart, in my opinion, is the most revealing piece of information one can have when trying to figure out whether a relationship is going to survive. Even though the synastry graph between two entities might be favorable, those types of charts won't show where the action lies and whether those two energy fields will operate in a harmonious or discordant manner.

The composite chart answers both dilemmas and puts to rest any speculation regarding the endurance or compatibility of two people or places. How many times have we seen couples whose planets were in harmony with us only to have the relationship turn sour when we became more than just casual friends or acquaintances? Conversely, I've known couples who had truly horrible synastry charts, yet the two had a mutually satisfying relationship for many years. When two energies combine, somehow those energies which appear to work on the surface could disintegrate in the final analysis, while other divergent forces seem to ignore the basic differences between themselves. It's all a matter of physics or chemistry. Some forces seem to attract while others repel.

To erect a composite chart between two, or more, entities, you must have an accurate birthchart, one for yourself and one for the place you're investigating. Even if you don't have a birthtime, you can still glean considerable information from the basic midpoints and the aspects of the planets. You may want to erect a noon chart for both parties when this dilemma occurs. For this section, I've again chosen the city of Las Vegas and compared it to the five individuals we've been studying.

Before you can erect a composite chart, however, you must do one very important thing. You must always calculate the composite chart from your relocated MC in a specific location; you cannot use your natal MC unless you're still living in the place of your birth. Until I started doing charts in this

manner, I was continually confused as to why my interpretation was out in left field. The action was falling into the wrong houses and my delineation made no sense whatsoever.

You may question my rationale for doing composite charts in this manner, so let me explain. You can't mix apples and oranges: your natal MC and the MC of a particular city (or person) are coming from differing perspectives. To decipher the truth, both parties have to be in the same place, scant information can be gleaned from looking at tourist brochures, one must feel the vibrations of a place before major changes can be analyzed. A person in New York won't feel the effects of Los Angeles until they move to lotus land. A person viewing the backside of a statue won't see what the person who's viewing the statue from the front side sees until they both move to a place where they see the same thing at the same time. Since cities don't relocate, the individual must relocate their chart instead.

Erecting composite charts in this manner explains why some relationships that prosper in one locale fall apart when both parties move to another place. After you've calculated your composite MC, then look into a table of houses to ascertain the appropriate ASC.

To calculate the composite MC for Liberace and Las Vegas, we do the following:

Liberace's relocated MC in Las Vegas is 2 Libra 36 or 182°36'. The natal MC for Las Vegas is 29 Aries 43 or 29°43'. Adding the two figures together gives 211°79' or 212°19'. Dividing by two gives 106°10'. This gives a composite MC of 16 Cancer 10. Looking in a table of houses, this gives an Ascendant of 14 Libra 30. Calculate the planets in the same manner. To save time, you may wish to order a composite chart from a major computer firm. Just make certain that you adjust your birthtime, if needed, by adding or subtracting the correct number of hours. For Liberace who was born at 11:15PM CWT, this becomes 10:15PM CST. Since Las Vegas is on PST, or two hours behind CST, Liberace's relocated birthtime thus becomes 8:15PM PST. Then place the composite planets into the composite wheel, using Porphyry house cusps, although that decision is up to you.

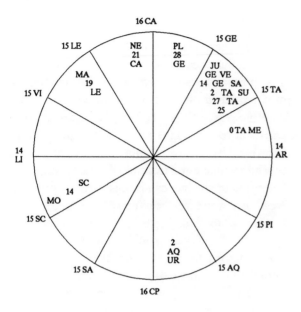

Figure 29. Composite Chart for Liberace and Las Vegas.

Using only a 3-degree orb, we'll look at the composite chart for Liberace and Las Vegas. We find two very fortunate and beneficial aspects to the angles: Moon trine MC and Jupiter trine ASC, both indicative of popularity and ability to make large sums of money. Since the Moon rules the composite MC and is placed in the second house of income, financial success is almost guaranteed. Another indication is the Sun in Taurus in the eighth house. Ordinarily, I wouldn't think of an eighth house Sun as being a portent of harmony, especially with a conjunction to Saturn. But Liberace did have Capricorn rising at birth so he could handle the nature of Saturn better than most people. Sun conjunct often toughens the weakest person or so thoroughly debilitates them they cannot perform the most basic task. This conjunction might also show the nature of his sex life which was hidden and kept secret from all but his closest associates.

Mercury sextiles Pluto but squares unpredictable Uranus. As Mercury rules the ninth and twelfth

houses and is places in the house of open enemies and adversaries (the seventh), one of several things might occur. Disgrace or embarrassment (twelfth) at the hands of a lover (seventh) possibly resulting in a lawsuit (ninth). Mercury's square to Uranus in the fifth of love and romance made this an even stronger possibility, especially since Uranus rules the fifth. We know the above came true soon before he passed away of AIDS. Venus trine Uranus also gave Liberace the ability to project himself with dramatic flair and extravagance.

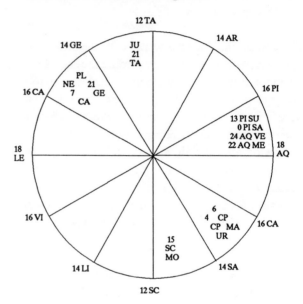

Figure 30. Composite Chart for Howard Hughes and Las Vegas.

In Hughes' chart, we find the Moon conjunct the IC and the Sun sextile the MC, two strong indications of success, security and fame. The Moon also squares the ASC so Hughes didn't enjoy speculation as to his comings and goings and tried to stay away from the prying eyes of the media as much as possible. Moon conjunct the IC wants peace and quiet more than anything, and Hughes hid in a cocoon protecting his privacy. Note that Jupiter's square to the ASC as well, indicating that Hughes often went overboard speculating (Jupiter rules the fifth) and might well have bought up the whole town had he lived there much longer.

Hughes composite Sun and Moon trine each other, unquestionably the best indication of harmony one could hope to find. Both luminaries in water signs again show the need for privacy and secrecy. Water signs usually don't reveal their intent or motivations to outsiders. Mercury, ruler of the second house, conjuncts Venus, ruler of the MC, another indication of wealth. Both square Jupiter in the tenth house so his reputation as a spendthrift or speculator put him in the headlines more frequently than he desired. His image was larger-than-life, something which Hughes did little to dispel.

Both Mercury and Venus trine Pluto indicating his transactions were hidden and kept from prying eyes. The suddenness of his appearance on the Las Vegas scene is shown by Mars and Uranus in the fifth house. A close associate once said that Hughes firmly believed that Vegas would one day become a seaport after California fell into the ocean. With Mars and Uranus opposing Neptune in Cancer, this "vision" doesn't seem all that unusual.

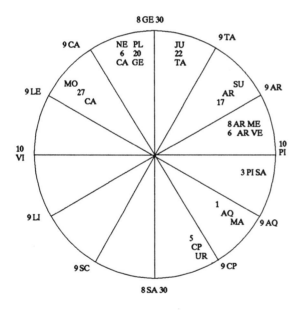

Figure 31. Composite Chart for Bugsy Siegel and Las Vegas.

Siegel's composite chart is another story altogether. The Sun in Aries indicates the tendency for pioneering and its sextile to Pluto in the 10th shows his involvement with the underworld. The ruler of the

composite ASC and MC (Mercury) sextiles the MC but inconjuncts the ASC: good on the business level but irritating on the personal. Venus sextile the MC made it easy for Siegel to get funding for his project (the Flamingo Hotel) as Venus rules the second house of finance.

Siegel's problems with laborers are shown by Uranus, ruler of the sixth house, inconjunct the MC. It's a miracle the Flamingo was completed at all with aspects like these due to the double-dealing of the workers. Mercury, ruler of the ASC and MC, squares Neptune, ruler of the DESC, which no doubt led to Siegel's assassination a year later.

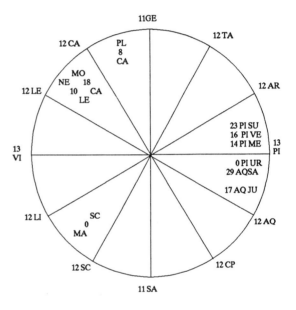

Figure 32. Composite Chart for Ken Ulston and Las Vegas.

Uston's composite chart is quite powerful, probably too powerful for his own good. Note that Neptune, ruler of the DESC, sextiles the MC indicating that other people would assist him in his ambition to "break the bank." But with a square from the ruler of the ASC and MC to Neptune, Uston's greed and often overbearing personality got in the way of progress, thus alienating those who could have assisted him when the chips were down. Note also that Venus, ruler of the second composite house,

101

opposes the ASC, meaning either pleasant times or open warfare.

Venus conjunct the DESC made it easy for Uston to pull the wool over the eyes of the casino bosses for some time due to its trine to the Moon, ruler of the eleventh house of friends. It's entirely possible that the dealers secretly wanted to see if Uston could outsmart the usual odds, but those managers looking through the mirrors in the ceiling above saw nothing but their profits going down the drain, thus Uston had to be stopped at all costs.

Mars, ruler of the eighth house of other people's money, trines Saturn and Uranus in the sixth house of work. Mars in the second is good for getting quick cash and the trines to those 6th house planets made it easier to try something radical or unexpected. The conjunction of Saturn and Uranus always produces stress and tension thus limiting their effectiveness.

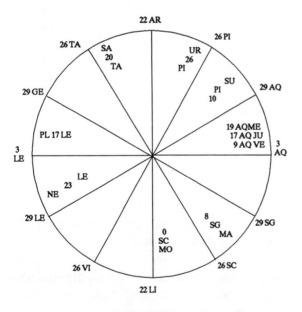

Figure 33. Composite Chart for Robert Urich and Las Vegas.

Robert Urich's composite chart is fraught with tension and frustration. Neptune, ruler of films and TV, trines the MC, so Urich did well when sticking to business. But the Moon square the ASC made

him feel like an outsider and produced little feeling of permanence or security, due to its rulership of the twelfth house. Urich's Sun square Mars showed that physical activity could benefit him in times of crisis but gave him little peace of mind where his children were concerned as Mars sits in the fifth house.

Mercury squares Saturn but conjuncts Jupiter, an odd combination which made his depression short-lived due to the inherent optimism of Jupiter, ruler of his natal Sun. Venus sextile Mars surrounded him with a sexual aura due to the role he played on screen. Since Venus rules the IC and Mars rules the MC, there was ironically little apparent conflict between his professional and private life. Jupiter square Saturn produces an easy come-easy go attitude, sort of a push-pull syndrome where there's often little real headway. Saturn square Neptune, however, doesn't bode well for good physical or emotional health, but Saturn's sextile to Pluto gave Urich strength to put up with adversity over the long haul.

As previously stated, the composite chart shows whether a relationship will survive over the long haul. For example, I know a couple who have 21 squares between their natal charts. They also have 5 trines, 9 sextiles, 1 opposition but only 1 conjunction, a total of only 14 positive aspects out of 37. It's a wonder their relationship ever got off the ground. But in their composite chart, the Sun, Mercury, Venus and Mars are conjunct within a few degrees, and all are trine Saturn, a clear indication of their long-lasting partnership. Their composite ASC is Aquarius, so first and foremost they are friends and give each other considerable freedom and independence.

I also believe that you can predict certain events from a composite chart. Transits of the outer planets often pinpoint periods of stress and adversity, while those of Jupiter show when good times are to be expected. The above-mentioned couple went through a couple years of adversity and near-calamity when Pluto squared their composite ASC. At the same time, Saturn was going over their composite MC, so life was no bed of roses for them. Not until transiting Jupiter sextiled their composite ASC did the period of stress fly out the window and both again became fully employed.

In my own personal life, while living in Chicago I had major surgery which required me to move to a more favorable climate when the ruler of my composite ASC conjuncted the ruler of my composite MC. By the time Uranus trined the composite ASC, I moved again from Florida to California where Uranus was conjuncting the composite IC.

In late 1988, Neptune was conjuncting my composite ASC in Los Angeles which created many disappointments and disillusionments about the quality of life in that city. Neptune often causes one to flee or to escape, which I did soon after to the Monterey Peninsula. The following year, transiting Uranus squared my composite MC causing many ups and downs in my career. As Uranus rules the eighth, life and death situations could come to the fore, which they did shortly before Christmas 1989 when I nearly died during an attack of double pneumonia. Having transiting Saturn and Neptune in the composite sixth house didn't help matters either and after four relapses, I finally decided to move to Hawaii. I left northern California the moment transiting Jupiter crossed my composite ASC and Neptune went into the seventh house.

SECTION IX

NUMEROLOGY AND RELOCATION

If you're one of those individuals who simply can't understand astrology or just prefers working with numbers, this part of my book should be of great value to you. Even though a complete numerological reading involves more concepts than I will delve into in this section, the abbreviated system I use for relocation is standard and can be found in most books on the subject.

I always use the complete name of a place, not just its first name, but the state as well. How could the post office expect to deliver a package to a place addressed only as Newark? Most numerologists don't agree with me on this, but from extensive research, my system is the one that works. After all, there's a great deal of difference between Portland, Maine, and Portland, Oregon, isn't there?

The most powerful vibration relates to the birthdate of a place or person. Unlike a name which may be changed at will through marriage, etc., the birthdate is fixed in stone, so to speak. But first, you'll have to agree that the birthdate of a city is accurate or this section of the book cannot be completed. Those dates shown in my book, *Horoscopes of the Western Hemisphere*, have proven time and time again to be accurate by me and most historians. The vibration which relates to the birthdate is called the DESTINY number. You find it as follows:

Las Vegas, Nevada, was founded on May 15, 1905. Add 5 for May plus 15 and 1905 which equals 1925. Then add 1,9,2 and 5 together which equals 17 and 1 plus 7 equals 8. The DESTINY number for Las Vegas is 8.

The second vibration pertains to the name of the place, including the state. For individuals, I don't believe the name you should use is the one listed on your birth certificate; use the name you are most comfortable being called. If you followed the "hard and fast" rule most numerologists advocate, how could you possibly give an accurate reading to someone who was adopted?

For example, some women prefer to use the name of their husband with Mrs. in front while others prefer to use their first name combined with their husband's last name. Mrs. George Bush has a different ring to it than does Mrs. Barbara Bush. People relate to you numerologically-speaking according to what they hear and the responses one gets is often directly related to the vibration one hears when first being introduced. Businessmen may use their initials, their first name and middle initial or their full name or a nickname. J.D. Smith, John D. Smith, John Davidson Smith and Jack Smith are all the same individual but the impression one forms when hearing these names differs considerably. It works the same for cities. Columbus, Ohio, gets a different feeling than does Columbus, Georgia, for example.

To compute the vibration of the name, add up the value of each letter from the following table:

1 = A,J,S   2 = B,K,T   3 = C,L,U   4 = D,M,V
5 = E,N,W   6 = F,O,X   7 = G,P,Y   8 = H,Q,Z
9 = I,R

For those born in countries where the Roman alphabet was not in use, you'll have to change your name to fit the above table. For cities in the western world, we don't have to worry about this. To find the numerological vibration of Las Vegas, Nevada, add up the value of each letter as shown above.

L A S V E G A S N E V A D A
3 1 1 4 5 7 1 1 5 5 4 1 4 1 = 43 and 4 + 3 = 7

Las Vegas' name vibration equals 7. This equals its EXPRESSION number.

Now we must separate the vowels from the consonants. The vowels are always A,E,I,O,U and Y if it happens to fall at the end of a word. Looking at Las Vegas' name, the vowel total is 14 or 1 + 4 = 5. The consonant total is 29 and 2 + 9 = 11 and 1 + 1 = 2.

Some numerologists might prefer to have the consonant total equal 11 as it corresponds to a higher vibration than does the number 2.

The vowel total corresponds to Las Vegas' HEART vibration. The consonant total corresponds to Las Vegas' PERSONALITY vibration. Add up the total for all vowels and consonants and they equal its EXPRESSION number which is 7.

Each number has a different meaning, depending on which book you happen to be reading. For relocation purposes, we're not concerned with the planetary vibration of each number, only whether the city's number vibrations in any way correspond to the vibrations in your own name or birthdate. For purposes of relocation, we'll be looking only at the HEART (vowel), EXPRESSION (vowel and consonant) and DESTINY (birthdate) numbers.

Numbers 1,2,4 and 8 are harmonious to one another.
Numbers 3,6 and 9 are compatible.
Numbers 5 and 7 operate on the same wavelength.

If you're a Number 8, for example, then try and find a place which has a Heart, Expression or Destiny number which equals 8. Second-best would be a place equaling 1,2 or 4. This series of numbers relates to the conjunction, opposition, square and semisquare astrologically-speaking. The 3,6 and 9 relate to the trine, sextile and novile while the 5 relates to the quintile and the 7 to the septile. You should steer clear of those places which have none of your personal numbers on their Heart, Expression or Destiny lines. To live in one of those places might make you feel out of place and continually out of sync.

Numerological compatibility may be achieved by the following:

1. Your HEART number and the HEART number of the city identical or in harmony with one another. This creates a great deal of understanding and you'll both have the same goals and desires.

2. Your EXPRESSION number and the EXPRESSION number of the city identical or in harmony. This facilitates cooperation and the people of that place appreciate your talents and abilities.

3. Your DESTINY numbers identical or in harmony. This means you and the city are going in the same direction, but not always using the same methods or at the same speed.

4. Your HEART number in harmony with the EXPRESSION number of the city. This means the city has something you want and will fulfill your deepest and most heartfelt desires.

5. Your EXPRESSION number in harmony with the city's HEART number shows this would be a good place to sell yourself, for the people will listen to you and agree with your ideas.

6. Your DESTINY number in harmony with the city's EXPRESSION number indicates this place is offering you considerable experience, whether you're in school, employed in the workforce or going through on-the-job training.

7. Your DESTINY number in harmony with the city's HEART number shows that this place makes you feel at home and you can "psych out" the people with ease. Life here is lived largely on the emotional or spiritual plane and it's a good place to make friends.

Now it's time to look at the numerological vibrations of our famous individuals who made a decided impact on Las Vegas.

	Heart	Expression	Destiny
Howard Hughes	6	2	6
Liberace	2	1	5
Bugsy Siegel	4	1	1
Robert Urich	5	2	6
Ken Uston	5	2	4
Las Vegas, Nevada	5	7	8

We see from the above comparison that Liberace's Heart and Expression numbers are in harmony with Las Vegas' Destiny number. Liberace's Destiny number is also in harmony with Las Vegas' Heart and Expression number. Four points of agreement.

Howard Hughes' Expression number harmonizes with Las Vegas' Destiny number. One point of agreement.

Bugsy Siegel's Heart, Expression and Destiny numbers are in harmony with Las Vegas' Destiny number. Three points of agreement.

Robert Urich's Heart number is identical to that of Las Vegas and his Expression number harmonizes with its Destiny number. Two points of agreement.

Ken Uston's Heart number is identical to that of Las Vegas, so they both wanted the same thing. Uston's Expression and Destiny numbers harmonize with Las Vegas' Destiny number. Three points of agreement.

Obviously the more points of agreement, the more one is drawn to a place or person. The following lists will give you the Heart, Expression and Destiny numbers for several American cities.

HEART NUMBERS (computed from the vowels)

1 = Phoenix, Ft. Lauderdale, Indianapolis, New Orleans, St. Louis, Dayton, Providence, Austin, Spokane, Cheyenne.

2 = Long Beach, San Diego, San Jose, Denver, Orlando, Honolulu, Albany NY, Toledo, Charleston SC, San Antonio, Milwaukee.

3 = Hartford, St. Petersburg, Baltimore, Detroit, Buffalo, Philadelphia, Houston.

4 = Chicago, Portland ME, Boston, New York, Cincinnati, Norfolk, Madison.

5 = Birmingham, Miami Beach, Des Moines, Las Vegas, Cleveland, Washington D.C.

6 = Mobile, Atlanta, Minneapolis, Omaha, Columbus OH, Portland OR, Tacoma.

7 = Los Angeles, Oakland, San Francisco, Memphis, Richmond VA.

8 = Miami, Louisville, St. Paul, Charlotte, Oklahoma City, Pittsburgh, Nashville, Dallas.

9 = Tampa, Kansas City MO, Reno, Albuquerque, Rochester NY, Tulsa, El Paso, Ft. Worth, Salt Lake City, Seattle.

EXPRESSION NUMBERS (vowel and consonant total)

1 = Hartford, Chicago, Boston, St. Louis, Omaha, Toledo, Philadelphia, Charleston SC, Nashville, Dallas, Houston, Salt Lake City.

2 = Long Beach, Oakland, Miami, New Orleans, Detroit, Kansas City MO, Oklahoma City, El Paso, San Antonio, Norfolk, Madison.

3 = San Francisco, Miami Beach, Louisville, Baltimore, Minneapolis, Buffalo, Portland OR, Tacoma.

4 = Phoenix, Indianapolis, Albany NY, Pittsburgh, Providence, Richmond VA, Spokane.

5 = Tucson, Atlanta, Tulsa, Ft. Worth, Seattle, Cheyenne, Washington D.C.

6 = Mobile, New York, Rochester NY.

7 = Denver, St. Petersburg, Honolulu, DEs Moines, Portland ME, St. Paul, Las Vegas, Charlotte.

8 = Birmingham, Los Angeles, Tampa, Albuquerque, Cincinnati, Cleveland.

9 = San Diego, San Jose, Ft. Lauderdale, Orlando, Reno, Columbus OH, Dayton, Memphis, Austin, Milwaukee.

DESTINY NUMBERS (computed from the birthdate)

1= Anchorage, Phoenix, Little Rock, San Diego, Colorado Spgs., Hartford, Savannah, Chicago, Louisville, Baltimore, Minneapolis, Reno, Charlotte, Cincinnati, Columbus OH, Dayton, Portland OR, Charleston SC, Memphis, Austin.

2 = Huntsville, Wilmington DE, Tampa, Boise, New Orleans, Columbia SC, Dallas, Cheyenne.

3 = Tucson, Los Angeles, Detroit, Jackson MS, Pittsburgh, Seattle, Spokane, Tacoma, Charleston WV.

4 = Atlanta, Lexington KY, Knoxville.

5 = Miami, Des Moines, Portland ME, Albuquerque, Rochester NY, Houston, San Antonio.

6 = Fresno, Sacramento, New Haven, Indianapolis, Cedar Rapids, Duluth, Albany NY, Syracuse, Salt Lake City, Norfolk.

7 = Denver, Jacksonville, Shreveport, St. Louis, Newark NJ, Akron, Cleveland, Oklahoma City, Tulsa, El Paso.

8 = Birmingham, Oakland, San Jose, Miami Beach, Honolulu, Ft. Wayne, Wichita, St. Paul, Kansas City MO, Las Vegas, Buffalo, Philadelphia, Nashville, Ft. Worth, Richmond, Madison.

9 = Mobile, Long Beach, San Francisco, Bridgeport, Orlando, St. Petersburg, Boston, Omaha, New York, Providence, Chattanooga, Milwaukee, Washington D.C.

108

SECTION X

BIORHYTHMS AND RELOCATION

We've now arrived at the final method I use when considering a spot for someone to relocate. The very nature of biorhythms often stretches one's credibility due to their total lack of scientific validation or research as to their effectiveness. I've read several books on the subject and looked at hundreds of graphs, and in my opinion, there's definitely something to biorhythms, but exactly what that thing is I can't ascertain. There does seem to be a lot of hidden, unseen or occult forces out there in our universe to which we tap into at the moment of our birth, some of which have been discovered in this century.

Your basic biorhythm numbers may be obtained from any number of books for sale at your local "new age" bookstore. For relocation purposes, we're not concerned with what those individual numbers mean. For that, I'll leave it up to experts like Irene Stephenson in Chatsworth, California. We'll be concentrating solely on the compatibility between your individual biorhythm numbers and those of a specific city. The dates used in this section are identical to those shown in my book, *Horoscopes of the Western Hemisphere*.

Biorhythms operate on three main levels: a 23-day physical cycle, a 28-day emotional cycle and a 33-day intellectual cycle. Each person has slightly different cycles due to the position of their Moon at birth and the length of gestation. My mentor, Dr. Van Courtland, did extensive research on the subject and could calculate within a few minutes when a line in a particular cycle crossed from the positive side to the negative. But for the purposes of this book, we'll use the average cycle.

After finding your initial biorhythm numbers, compare them to the numbers of the place you've selected for business or residence. Compatibility is measured according to how far those numbers are from each other. For example, the numbers for Los Angeles are 01-08-08. My biorhythm numbers are

12-23-11. The difference between them is computed as follows:

	Physical	Emotional	Intellectual
Los Angeles	01	08	08
Marc Penfield	12	23	11

The difference is   11 days   15 days   3 days

Now go to Table I to ascertain the degree of compatibility.

Between myself and Los Angeles, there's only 4 percent physical harmony, only 7 percent emotional harmony but a whopping 82 percent intellectual rapport. Now divide the sum total of percentages by three to get the overall compatibility or harmony. Anything between 60-80 percent is ideal; below that range could be quite disappointing at times while higher figures could lead to boredom with little impetus for change or adventure.

Now we'll look at the biorhythm compatibility for our five examples. The biorhythm numbers for Las Vegas are 18-22-07.

Howard Hughes numbers are 02-23-15 yielding 39 percent physical harmony, 93 percent emotional harmony and 52 percent intellectual rapport.

Liberace's numbers are 10-04-30 yielding 30 percent physical harmony, 29 percent emotional harmony and 39 percent intellectual rapport.

Bugsy Siegel's numbers are 05-13-15 yielding 13 percent physical harmony, 36 percent emotional harmony and 52 percent intellectual rapport.

Robert Urich's numbers are 05-05-27 yielding 13 percent physical harmony, 21 percent emotional harmony and only 21 percent intellectual rapport.

Ken Uston's numbers are 17-01-30 yielding 91 percent physical harmony, 50 percent emotional harmony and 39 percent intellectual rapport.

The overall harmony for the above people with Las Vegas is 94 percent for Hughes, 33 percent for

Liberace, 34 percent for Siegel, 18 percent for Urich and 60 percent for Uston. Hughes and Uston are the only two which had a strong rapport with this city, despite their divergent lifestyles.

From initial investigation it appears that the physical cycle is cardinal, the emotional is fixed and the intellectual is mutable. If one cycle is measurable higher than the other, that area of life will be more synchronized with your basic nature. In my case, with a high degree of intellectual compatibility here in Los Angeles, my life here has been involved with books, research and writing. The physical and em-otional side of my life has ofttimes left something to be desired. My overall harmony with this city is only 31 percent. My compatibility with Las Vegas is 48 percent physical, 93 percent emotional and 76 percent intellectual, which gives an overall harmony of 72 percent, which surprises me considering the number of times I've "lost my cool" in that town.

Biorhythms cannot be considered by themselves, only as a small piece of the puzzle which involves other types of charts and graphs already shown in this book.

TABLE I. BIORHYTHM COMPATIBILITY

PHYSICAL		EMOTIONAL		INTELLECTUAL	
Days Apart	/Harmony	Days Apart	/Harmony	Days Apart	/Harmony
0	100%	0	100%	0	100%
1	91	1	93	1	94
2	83	2	86	2	88
3	74	3	79	3	82
4	65	4	71	4	76
5	56	5	63	5	70
6	48	6	57	6	64
7	39	7	50	7	58
8	30	8	43	8	52
9	22	9	36	9	46
10	13	10	29	10	39
11	4	11	21	11	33
12	4	12	14	12	27
13	13	13	7	13	21
14	22	14	0	14	15
15	30	15	7	15	9
16	39	16	14	16	3
17	48	17	21	17	3
18	56	18	29	18	9
19	65	19	36	19	15
20	74	20	43	20	21
21	83	21	50	21	27
22	91	22	57	22	33
23	100%	23	64	23	39
		24	71	24	46
		25	79	25	52
		26	86	26	58
		27	93	27	64
		28	100%	28	70
				29	76
				30	82
				31	88
				32	94
				33	100%

TABLE II. BIORHYTHM NUMBERS FOR AMERICAN CITIES

ALABAMA

Birmingham	10-05-27	Mobile	14-01-20
Montgomery	16-11-31		

ALASKA

Anchorage	20-16-30	Fairbanks	09-22-20
Juneau	16-03-09		

ARIZONA

Phoenix	16-19-26	Tucson	22-02-03

ARKANSAS

Fort Smith	18-20-14	Little Rock	12-21-02

CALIFORNIA

Anaheim	08-04-01	Bakersfield	14-12-16
Berkeley	16-05-19	Fresno	01-22-02
Long Beach	03-14-19	Los Angeles	01-08-08
Monterey	17-02-26	Oakland	03-05-30
Palm Springs	05-14-09	Sacramento	22-14-32
San Diego	18-17-19	San Francisco	10-27-22
San Jose	19-11-30	Santa Barbara	01-02-09

COLORADO

Boulder	08-05-06	Colorado Spgs.	08-15-06
Denver	17-22-08	Pueblo	08-03-28

CONNECTICUT

Bridgeport	14-10-03	Hartford	16-18-22
New Haven	19-14-03	Waterbury	05-07-16

DELAWARE

Dover	20-03-10	Wilmington	09-27-16

FLORIDA

Daytona Beach	20-07-11	Ft. Lauderdale	08-25-19
Gainesville	11-00-01	Jacksonville	11-10-30
Key West	21-18-13	Miami	15-27-16
Miami Beach	10-13-08	Orlando	19-23-05
Pensacola	21-15-22	St. Petersburg	22-20-04
Tallahassee	05-27-30	Tampa	09-06-17

GEORGIA

Atlanta	10-11-19	Augusta	04-05-25
Columbus	17-08-25	Macon	20-27-15
Savannah	04-20-23		

HAWAII

Hilo	13-02-28	Honolulu	04-25-32

IDAHO

Boise	13-24-18	Idaho Falls	14-20-01
Lewiston	03-07-21		

ILLINOIS

Chicago	11-27-10	Evanston	11-18-15

Peoria	14-15-28	Rockford	20-09-32
Springfield	06-22-00	Urbana	19-00-22

INDIANA

Bloomington	20-25-06	Evansville	18-19-01
Fort Wayne	11-27-29	Gary	09-04-16
Indianapolis	14-21-10	South Bend	00-22-23
Terre Haute	01-26-11		

IOWA

Cedar Rapids	01-00-32	Davenport	22-06-07
Des Moines	03-10-09	Iowa City	19-22-05
Sioux City	19-03-17	Waterloo	19-05-12

KANSAS

Kansas City	06-02-03	Topeka	18-21-16
Wichita	18-04-04		

KENTUCKY

Frankfort	06-00-07	Lexington	10-05-21
Louisville	00-27-15	Owensboro	11-18-29
Paducah	22-24-06		

LOUISIANA

Baton Rouge	16-08-27	Monroe	21-20-16
New Orleans	10-12-25	Shreveport	08-06-18

MAINE

Augusta	10-26-09	Bangor	12-18-11
Lewiston	22-18-24	Portland	22-08-12

MARYLAND

Annapolis	09-16-04	Baltimore	21-14-18
Cumberland	11-19-31		

MASSACHUSETTS

Boston	08-14-03	Cambridge	11-14-23
Lawrence	07-21-00	Pittsfield	13-01-24
Springfield	03-11-17	Worcester	09-07-04

MICHIGAN

Ann Arbor	01-18-16	Detroit	07-10-32
Flint	00-18-17	Grand Rapids	06-19-32
Kalamazoo	16-10-06	Lansing	10-14-32
Saginaw	10-01-03		

MINNESOTA

Duluth	10-16-07	Minneapolis	09-10-15
Rochester	03-27-30	Saint Paul	17-16-14

MISSISSIPPI

Biloxi	12-08-17	Gulfport	03-00-26
Jackson	07-17-02	Meridian	02-21-19
Natchez	21-23-20	Vicksburg	10-21-11

MISSOURI

Columbia	11-09-25	Jefferson City	17-09-32
Joplin	10-17-08	Kansas City	08-26-22
Saint Louis	19-08-18	Springfield	14-17-01

MONTANA

Billings	14-08-06	Butte	17-06-04
Great Falls	09-24-13	Helena	13-17-30
Missoula	14-23-08		

NEBRASKA

Grand Island	20-04-32	Lincoln	06-18-16
North Platte	08-04-15	Omaha	04-00-31

NEVADA

Carson City	10-20-13	Las Vegas	18-22-07
Reno	14-18-30		

NEW HAMPSHIRE

Concord	21-11-03	Portsmouth	21-02-01

NEW JERSEY

Atlantic City	19-18-29	Camden	16-15-02
Jersey City	03-09-31	Newark	12-25-01
Trenton	10-24-17		

NEW MEXICO

Albuquerque	03-02-22	Las Cruces	16-01-19
Roswell	19-24-23	Santa Fe	09-27-24

NEW YORK

Albany	09-10-15	Binghamton	14-14-32
Buffalo	15-08-24	Elmira	16-00-30
New York City	06-03-04	Niagara Falls	21-09-01
Rochester	11-04-01	Schenectady	10-04-25
Syracuse	10-20-31	Utica	01-03-28

NORTH CAROLINA

Asheville	14-10-24	Chapel Hill	16-12-11
Charlotte	10-05-07	Durham	09-22-11
Greensboro	22-11-25	Raleigh	22-06-03
Winston-Salem	11-25-30		

NORTH DAKOTA

Bismarck	20-08-16	Fargo	15-17-03
Grand Forks	01-07-09	Minot	21-10-18

OHIO

Akron	07-01-15	Canton	19-19-15
Cincinnati	20-24-09	Cleveland	17-05-18
Columbus	14-05-10	Dayton	14-05-31
Springfield	00-17-05	Toledo	16-04-11
Youngstown	01-03-10		

OKLAHOMA

Lawton	16-00-32	Muskogee	14-00-16
Oklahoma City	19-08-32	Tulsa	14-08-06

OREGON

Eugene	08-08-07	Medford	14-26-02
Portland	13-04-00	Salem	06-02-04

PENNSYLVANIA

Altoona	00-01-22	Erie	13-18-22

Harrisburg	03-07-26	Johnstown	16-08-04
Lancaster	21-22-11	Philadelphia	08-10-11
Pittsburgh	16-10-10	Scranton	04-00-21

RHODE ISLAND

Newport	04-23-16	Providence	08-26-32

SOUTH CAROLINA

Charleston	16-03-31	Columbia	19-27-30
Greenville	22-25-07	Spartanburg	17-06-26

SOUTH DAKOTA

Aberdeen	15-16-28	Pierre	20-16-23
Rapid City	18-26-20	Sioux Falls	07-09-32

TENNESSEE

Chattanooga	18-06-07	Knoxville	22-22-22
Memphis	04-10-28	Nashville	16-02-11

TEXAS

Amarillo	22-21-06	Austin	02-00-11
Beaumont	13-04-19	Corpus Christi	15-09-19
Dallas	11-06-20	El Paso	09-14-01
Fort Worth	09-15-08	Galveston	12-13-21
Houston	03-07-28	Laredo	18-12-13
Lubbock	11-18-20	San Antonio	22-16-11
Waco	08-27-10	Wichita Falls	01-06-20

UTAH

Logan	15-14-07	Ogden	06-19-26
Provo	20-16-32	Salt Lake City	18-24-01

VERMONT

Burlington	20-06-17	Montpelier	20-18-29

VIRGINIA

Alexandria	01-06-23	Charlottesville	22-05-06
Hampton	13-15-09	Lynchburg	21-07-14
Newport News	00-06-14	Norfolk	12-27-07
Portsmouth	06-09-25	Richmond	04-14-24
Roanoke	01-02-22	Virginia Beach	13-28-11

WASHINGTON

Olympia	00-15-14	Seattle	09-19-12
Spokane	11-06-26	Tacoma	08-20-05
Tacoma	19-04-12		

WEST VIRGINIA

Charleston	08-13-19	Parkersburg	04-01-02

WISCONSIN

Green Bay	10-15-13	Kenosha	11-04-11
La Crosse	09-08-06	Madison	03-27-02
Milwaukee	02-05-22	Oshkosh	21-12-10
Racine	15-19-24		

WYOMING

Casper	09-12-14	Cheyenne	12-12-07
Laramie	14-18-30	Rock Springs	15-06-28

DISTRICT OF COLUMBIA
Washington   12-00-26

TABLE III. BIORHYTHM NUMBERS FOR CANADIAN CITIES

ALBERTA

Calgary	01-20-12	Edmonton	21-10-11

BRITISH COLUMBIA

Vancouver	04-00-22	Victoria	01-21-10

MANITOBA

Winnipeg	00-03-10

NEW BRUNSWICK

Fredericton	06-23-32	Saint John	08-10-21

NEWFOUNDLAND

Saint John's	04-22-10

NOVA SCOTIA

Halifax	00-00-12

ONTARIO

Ottawa	11-10-12	Toronto	01-01-17

PRINCE EDWARD ISLAND

Charlottetown	06-02-05

QUEBEC

Montreal	03-10-00	Quebec City	01-06-30

SASKATCHEWAN

Regina	18-12-10	Saskatoon	00-10-27

YUKON TERRITORY

Dawson	13-22-31	Whitehorse	20-08-08

POSTSCRIPT

YOUR FINAL CHOICE

At this point, readers of this book will fall into one of three categories:

GROUP I: Individuals who will have little say-so with regards to relocation, the decision having already been made for them by someone else, be it their employer, parent or spouse. About the only free will they have is to try and understand what life has in store for them in their new place of residence and how their perspective and outlook may change in the process.

GROUP II: Individuals who have two or three choices at most. With the possibility of a better job or a more promising relationship requires them to look over only a limited number of locations. Many of them may, in the end, decide to stay where they are, especially if that job offer or romantic liaison doesn't pan out as originally planned.

GROUP III: Individuals who have been granted unlimited funds or free time to make their final decision. Life has given them "carte blanche" and places few pressures on them to make up their mind in record time. Often these are self-employed individuals with minimal ties to the community and are not involved in a current relationship. They have the privilege of packing up and leaving whenever the mood strikes them.

Those in Group I will have only one city to investigate. A few might quit their job rather than make an unwanted transfer, but most are at the mercy of someone else's decision. Those in Group II have the task of picking and choosing whether to stay put or to move. They're saddled with only a few options and in a way are the luckiest group of all. However, there's a time limit involved lest one miss opportunities offered right now. Those in Group III will have the hardest lot of all. With their ability to pick and choose at will, they've saddled themselves with a considerable responsibility if their final decision is to be sensibly made.

After looking at all the divergent types of charts and graphs in this book, some readers may still be in a quandary. The basic relocation chart, computed from one's original birthtime, is the most important one to consider. After all, this type of chart illustrates the amount of free will you will have in a given locale. The geodetic and declination charts show only the impact the environment will have on an individual and should be carefully scrutinized after looking at the basic relocation chart. For those without an accurate birthtime, however, the geodetic and declination charts are more important than usual.

The synastry and composite charts are also important, but as mentioned earlier, they illustrate only in the most general terms the compatibility between an individual and a city. The beauty of these types of charts, however, is that one often finds where the action lies and thus the focus of your life in that particular place.

Many readers will note radical differences between their basic relocation, geodetic and declination charts. What initially might appear as a "green light" upon further investigation could prove more than the individual might care to endure. A "red light" that upon first analysis presented the individual with too many challenges or frustrations could in the long run to be more favorable than originally anticipated. In the end, there's no hard and fast rule to consider when contemplating relocation. Each individual's needs and requirements are different, but if you look long enough, I'm certain you'll find a place that fits all your parameters.

In a philosophical sense, those of us in the western world have been taught that the individual is paramount and independent thought and action play a major role in our lives. Eastern philosophy by contrast teaches that the individual is nothing more than a small part of the whole to which we must conform if we are to live in harmony. The truth, obviously, lies somewhere in between.

Some considerations should also be noted which are beyond the scope of this book. Factors which relate to the economy, cost of living, tax structure, manufacturing and industrial base are better obtained from government publications. Some will want to know the religious, cultural, ethnic or racial background before they make their final decision. Individuals with families will want to know about the quality of education, day care facilities and cost of buying a home. All of want to know whether a location has a crime rate that's gone through the ceiling as that one fact threatens our basic security and safety more than any other single fact. For some, however, their only consideration will be the climate, all else being fair game.

One final word of warning. For those well-versed in transits and progressions, you should always look at your progressed chart to see if relocation is advised during the current year. Failure to do this could mean the difference between success and failure, not to mention being in the right place at the wrong time. There are places where one's progressions will be more favorable than others for a designated period of time, but after a few years or so, conditions will change and new patterns emerge.

All an astrologer, or the reader, can be expected to do is to point out the pros and cons of choosing one specific place over another. You're totally responsible for the final decision, unless you happen to fall in Group I. After all, no place on earth is entirely free from adversity and no place is perfect. A few sacrifices or compromises will have to be made irrespective of where one decides to live. With this in mind, I wish you the best of luck and hope that you find your ideal location where you can grab the reins of happiness, success and prosperity. BON VOYAGE!

BIBLIOGRAPHY

RELOCATION

Baigent, Michael et al. *Mundane Astrology*. Northamptonshire: Aquarian Press, 1984.

Cozzi, Steve. *Planets in Locality*. St. Paul: Llewellyn Books, 1988.

Dobyns, Zipporah. *Working With Local Space*. San Diego: ACS Publications, 1987.

Lewis, Jim, Astro*Carto*Graphy Maps, PO Box 959, El Cerrito, CA 94530.

Lewis, Jim. and Ariel Guttman. *Astro*Carto*Graphy Book of Maps*. San Diego: ACS Publications, 1989.

Pottenger, Maritha. *Astrolocality Maps*. San Diego: ACS Publications.

Warren, D. *Your Best Place*. Hoboken, NY: 9th Sign Books, 1978.

COMPOSITES

Campion, Nicholas. *Book of World Horoscopes*. Northamptonshire: Aquarian Press, 1988.

Dodson, Carolyn. *Horoscopes of U.S. Cities*. San Diego: ACS Publications, 1975.

Hand, Robert. *Planets in Composite*. Rockport, ME: Para Research, 1975.

Penfield, Marc. *Horoscopes of the Western Hemisphere*. San Diego: ACS Publications, 1984.

SYNASTRY

Davidson, Ronald. *Synastry*. New York: ASI Publications

Sakoian, Frances, and Louis Acker. *Astrology of Human Relationships*. New York: Harper & Row, 1976.

ASPECTS

Pelletier, Robert. *Planets in Aspect*, Rockport, ME: Para Research 1974.

Sakoian, Frances, and Louis Acker, *The Astrologer's Handbook*. New York: Harper & Row, 1973.

BIORHYTHMS

Thommen, George. *Is This Your Day?* New York: Avon Books, 1976.

NUMEROLOGY

Gruner, Mark. *Numbers of Life*. New York: Taplinger Books, 1978.

Vaughn, Richard. *Numbers as Symbols of Self-Discovery*. Reno, NV: CRSC Publications, 1985.

GEODETIC CHARTS

Johndro, E.L. *The Earth in the Heavens*. New York: Samuel Weiser, 1973.

Johndro, E.L. *The Stars*. New York: Samuel Weiser, 1973.

McEvers, Joan, ed. *Astrology of the Macrocosm*. St. Paul: Llewellyn Books, 1990.

DATA SOURCE BOOKS

Barbault, Andre. *Le Zodiaque*. Paris, 1968.

Clark, Katherine, et al. *Comtemporary Sidereal Horoscopes*. San Francisco: Sidereal Research Publishing, 1976.

Doane, Doris Chase. *Horoscopes of U.S. Presidents*. Hollywood, CA: PAI Publications, 1971.

Drew, Marion Meyer. *101 Headline Horoscopes*, New York, 1941.

------. *101 Hard to Find Horoscopes*. New York, 1962.

Gauquelin, Michel & Francoise. *Book of American Charts*. San Diego, ACS Publications, 1982.

------. *Birth Data (6 Vols.)*. Paris, 1970.

Hammitt, Howard. *Chronological Nativities*. San Francisco, 1970.

Jones, Marc Edmund. *Sabian Symbols*. Stanwood, WA: Sabian Press, 1953.

Leo, Alan. *1001 Notable Nativities*. London: Fowler, 1917.

More Notable Nativities. Chicago: Aries Press.

Rodden, Lois. *American Book of Charts*. Tempe, AZ: AFA, 1980.

------. *Astro Data III*. Tempe, AZ: AFA, 1983.

------. *Astro Data IV*. Tempe, AZ: AFA, 1990.

------. *Profiles of Women*. Tempe, AZ: AFA, 1979.

------. *Data News*. P. O. Box 1613, Hollywood, CA 90078.

Wemyss, Maurice, *Famous Nativities*. London, 1938.

DATA SOURCES

ADAMS, ANSEL: San Francisco CA, Feb 20, 1902, 3AM, from autobiog.

ADDAMS, JANE: Cedarville IL, Sept 6, 1860, 3:39AM LMT, from SS.

ADENAUER, KONRAD: Bonn, Ger., Jan 5, 1876, 10:30AM LMT, from Gau.

ALBERT, PRINCE: Rosenau, Ger., Aug 26, 1819, 6AM LMT, from SS.

ALEXANDRA, Darmstadt, Ger., Jun 6, 1872, 3:45AM LMT, from Archive.

ALLRED, GLORIA: Philadelphia PA, Jul 3, 1941, 10PM, per mother.

ANNE, QUEEN: London, Eng., Feb 16, 1665, 11:39PM, per bio. by Green.

ANN-MARGRET: Valsjobyn, Swe., Apr 28, 1941, 4:30AM, from herself.

ARBUCKLE, FATTY: Smith Center KS, Mar 24, 1887, 7:50AM CST, from SS.

AUGUSTUS: Rome, Italy, Sep 22, 63BC, sunrise, per Suetonius.

BAKER, JOSEPHINE: St. Louis MO, Jun 3, 1906, 11AM CST (bio. Bouillon).

BAKKER, JIM: Muskegon Hts MI, Jan 2, 1940, 11AM EST, per BC.

BALL, LUCILLE: Jamestown NY, Aug 6, 1911, 4AM EST, from MMD.

BALZAC, HONORE DE: Tours, Fr., May 20, 1799, 11AM LMT, from Gau.

BARDOT, BRIGITTE: Paris, Fr., Sep 28, 1934, 1:15PM, from Gau

BARNARD, CHRISTIAAN: Beaufort West, SA, Nov 8, 1922, 8PM MET, from autobiog.

BARR, ROSEANNE: Salt Lake City UT, Nov 3, 1952, 1:21PM MST, per BC.

BARRYMORE, JOHN: Philadelphia PA, Feb 15, 1882, noon LMT, from SS.

BARTHOLDI, F.A.: Colmar, Fr., Apr 2, 1834, 6:30AM LMT, from Gau. (Date has been corrected.)

BARTON, CLARA: Oxford MA, Dec 25, 1821, noon LMT, from SS.

BEATTY, WARREN: Richmond VA, Mar 30, 1837, 5:30PM, per BC.

BECKER, BORIS: Leimen, Ger., Nov 22, 1967, 8:45AM MET, per BC.

BEETHOVEN, LUDWIG VAN: Bonn, Ger., Dec 16, 1770, 1:29PM LMT, per Kraum.

BELL, ALEXANDER GRAHAM: Edinburgh, Scot., Mar 3, 1847, 7AM LMT, per BC.

BELLI, MELVIN: Sonora CA, Jul 29, 1907, 8AM, in a letter.

BELUSHI, JOHN: Chicago IL, Jan 25, 1949, 5:12AM CST, per BC.

BEN GURION, DAVID: Plonsk, Pol., Oct 16, 1886, 12:42PM LMT, from Ebertin.

BENNETT, MICHAEL: Buffalo NY, Apr 8, 1943, 8AM, from BC.

BERGMAN, INGRID: Stockholm, Swe., Aug 29, 1915, 3:30AM, from BR.

BERLIN, IRVING: Tyumen, Rus., May 11, 1888, 8AM LMT, from MMD. (Chart corrected as original coordinates were in error.)

BISMARCK, OTTO VON: Schoenhausen, Ger., Apr 1, 1815, 1:30PM LMT. (Birth recorded between 1-2PM.)

BLAVATSKY, HELENA: Dnieperpetrovsk, Rus., Aug 12, 1831, 2:17AM LMT, from SS.

BLIGH, WILLIAM: Plymouth, Eng., Sep 9, 1754, 1AM LMT, from Bible.

BOLIVAR, SIMON: Caracas, Ven., Jul 24, 1783, 10PM, per family records.

BONHEUR, ROSA: Bordeaux, Fr., Mar 16, 1822, 8PM, per autobiog.

BORDEN, LIZZIE: Fall River MA, Jul 19, 1860, 10AM, per family records.

BORMANN, MARTIN: Halberstadt, Ger., Jun 17, 1900, 11:30PM, from Gau.

BOYCE, CHRISTOPHER: Santa Monica CA, Feb 16, 1953, 2:01PM PST, per BC.

BRADBURY, RAY: Waukegan IL, Aug 22, 1920, 4:50PM CWT, per BC.

BRAHMS, JOHANNES: Hamburg, Ger., May 7, 1833, 3:30AM LMT, per Kraum.

BRANDO, MARLON: Omaha NB, Apr 3, 1924, 11PM CST, per BC.

BRAUN, EVA: Munich, Ger., Feb 6, 1912, 12:30AM, per BC.

BROWN, HELEN GURLEY: Green Forest AR, Feb 18, 1922, 3AM CST, per BC.

BROWNING, ELIZABETH: Durham, Eng., Mar 6, 1806, 7PM LMT, from SS.

BRUCE, LENNY: Mineola NY, Oct 13, 1925, 11:24AM EST, per BC.

BRYAN, WM. J.: Salem IL, Mar 19, 1860, 9:04AM LMT, from SS.

BRYANT, ANITA, Barnsdall OK, Mar 25, 1940, 3:10PM CST, per BC.

BRYNNER, YUL: Vladivostok, Rus., Jul 11, 1920, 6:15AM LMT, from himself.

BUCK, PEARL: Hillsboro WV, Jun 26, 1892, 12:30AM EST, (biog. Harris)

BUNDY, THEODORE: Burligton VT, Nov 24, 1946, 10:35PM EST, per BC.

BURNETT, CAROL: San Antonio TX, Apr 26, 1933, 4AM CST, per BC.

BURTON, RICHARD: Pontrhydyfen, Wales, Nov 10, 1925, 5:30AM GMT. (Biography by his brother says between 5-5:30AM.)

BURTON, SIR RICHARD: Torquay, Eng., Mar 19, 1821, 9:30PM LMT, from SS.

BUSH, BARBARA: Rye NY, Jun 8, 1925, 7PM, from Zip Dobyns.

BUSH, GEORGE: Milton MA, Jun 12, 1924, 11:30AM EDT, mother says between 11AM and noon.

BYRON, LORD: London, Eng., Jan 22, 1788, 2PM LMT, per NN.

CABRINI, MOTHER: Lodi, Italy, Jul 15, 1850, 7:07AM, from CL.

CAPONE, AL: Brooklyn NY, Jan 17, 1899, 6AM EST, per MMD.

CAPOTE, TRUMAN: New Orleans LA, Sep 30, 1924, 3PM CST. (biog. Clarke)

CARNEGIE, ANDREW: Dunfermline, Scot., Nov 25, 1835, 6AM LMT, from SS. (Chart was incorrectly erected for 4AM.)

CARTER, JIMMY: Plains GA, Oct 1, 1924, 7AM CST, from AFA.

CARTER, ROSALYNN: Plains GA, Aug 18, 1927,6AM, from Family Circle.

CARTLAND, BARBARA: Edgebaston, Eng., Jul 9, 1901,11:40AM from her

CARUSO, ENRICO: Naples, Italy, Feb 27, 1873, 3AM LMT, from Gau.

CASALS, PABLO: Vendrell, Spain, Dec 30, 1876, 8PM LMT, per BC.

CASSATT, MARY: Pittsburgh PA, May 22, 1844, 11:55PM LMT, per family records.

CASTRO, FIDEL: Biran, Cuba, Aug 13, 1927, 2AM EST. (biog. Bourne)

CATHERINE OF ARAGON,Alcala, Spain, Dec 16, 1485, 2:30PM LMT, from royal archives which state mid-afternoon.

CATHERINE THE GREAT, Stettin, Pol., May 2, 1729, 2:30AM LMT. (Biog. Kaus)

CAYCE, EDGAR: Hopkisville KY, Mar 18, 1877, 3:30PM LMT, from SS.

CELLINI, BENVENUTO: Florence, Italy, Nov 2, 1500, 9PM LMT, from father's diary.

CHAMBERLAIN, NEVILLE: Birmingham, Eng., Mar 18, 1869, 1AM LMT, from BC.

CHAMBERLAIN, RICHARD: Los Angeles CA, Mar 31, 1934, 6:20PM, per BC.

CHANEL, COCO: Saumur, Fr., Aug 19, 1883, 4PM, per Gau.

CHANNING, CAROL: Seattle WA, Jan 31, 1921, 9PM PST, per BC.

CHAPLIN, CHARLES: London, Eng., Apr 16, 1889, 8PM GMT, per autobiog.

CHARLES I: Dunfermline, Scot., Nov 29, 1600, 10PM LMT, per NN.

CHARLES, PRINCE: London, Eng., Nov 14, 1948, 9:14PM GMT, per London Times.

CHER: El Centro CA, May 20, 1946, 7:31AM PST, per BC.

CHIANG KAI-SHEK,Ningpo, China, Oct 31, 1887, noon LMT, per MMD

CHOPIN, FREDRIC: Zelazowa Wola, Pol., Feb 22, 1810, 6PM LMT, from SS.

CHURCHILL, WINSTON: Blenheim, Eng., Nov 30, 1874, 1:30AM LMT, from father's diary.

CLIBURN, VAN: Shreveport LA, Jul 12, 1934, 11:45AM CST, from BC.

COLLINS, JOAN: London, Eng., May 23, 1933, 7AM BST.(biog. *Hollywood Sisters* by Crimp and Burstein)

COOK, CAPT. JAMES: Malton, Eng., Nov 7, 1728, :15AM LMT, from Dell.

COOLIDGE, CALVIN: Plymouth VT, Jul 4, 1872, 9AM, per SS.

COPPOLA, FRANCIS F.: Detroit MI, Apr 7, 1939, 1:38AM EST, per BC.

CRAWFORD, JOAN: San Antonio TX, Mar 23, 1903, 10PM CST, from CL.

CRONKHITE, WALTER: St. Joseph MO, Nov 4, 1916, 6AM CST, per BC.

CURIE, MARIE: Warsaw, Pol., Nov 7, 1867, noon per BC.

DAMIEN, JOSEPH: Tremelo, Bel., Jan 3, 1840, 1PM LMT, from Le Verseau magazine which says 12:30PM, chart rectified.

DARWIN, CHARLES: Shrewsbury, Eng., Feb 12, 1809, 6AM LMT, from AA.

DAVIES, MARION: Brooklyn NY, Jan 3, 1897, 6AM, per autobio.

DA VINCI, LEONARDO: Vinci, Italy, Apr 15, 1452, 10PM LMT, from father's diary.

DAVIS, BETTE: Lowell MA, Apr 5, 1908, 11:50PM EST, from SS.

DEAN, JAMES: Marion IN, Feb 8, 1931, 9:09PM CST, per BC.

DE GAULLE, CHARLES: Lille, Fr., Nov 22, 1890, 4PM per Gau.

DE LOREAN, JOHN: Detroit MI, Jan 6, 1925, noon EST, per BC.

DE MILLE, CECIL B.: Ashfield MA, Aug 12, 1881, 5:14AM LMT, from CL.

DENG XIAO PING: Guangan, China, Aug 22, 1904, 8:30PM LMT.(from Hong Kong 1997 by Ted Gormick)

DE VALERA, EAMON: New York NY, Oct 14, 1882, 5:11PM LMT, from SS.

DILLINGER, JOHN: Mooresville IN, Jun 22, 1903, 11:50PM CST. (biog. Cromie)

DIOR, CHRISTIAN: Granville, Fr. Jan 21, 1905, 1:30AM, per BC.

DISNEY, WALT: Chicago IL, Dec 5, 1901, 12:30AM CST, from SS.

DISRAELI, BENJAMIN: London, Eng., Dec 21, 1804, 5:30AM LMT, from SS.

DONAHUE, PHIL: Cleveland OH, Dec 21, 1930, 11:25AM EST, per BC.

DOOLEY, Dr. TOM: St. Louis MO. Jan 17, 1927, 2:20AM CST, per BC.

DOYLE, ARTHUR CONAN: Edinburgh, Scot., May 22, 1859, 4:55AM, per BC.

DU BARRY, MME: Vaucouleurs, Fr., Aug 19, 1743, 7:30AM, from Fagan

DUMAS, ALEXANDRE: Villiers, Fr., Jul 24, 1802, 5:30AM LMT, from Gau.

EARHART, AMELIA: Atchisn KS, Jul 24, 1897, 11:30PM CST, from AA.

EDDY, MARY BAKER: Bow NH, Jul 16, 1821, 5:33PM LMT, from SS.

EDISON, THOMAS: Milan OH, Feb 11, 1847, 3AM LMT, from an old biog.

EDWARD VII, London, Eng., Nov 9, 1841, 10:48AM, per NN

EICHMANN, ADOLPH: Solingen, Ger., Mar 19, 1906, 9AM MET, per BC.

EISENHOWER, DWIGHT: Denison TX, Oct 14, 1890, 5:45PM CST, from DCD

EISENHOWER, MAMIE: Boone IA, Nov 14, 1896, 1PM, from AA.

ELIZABETH I: Greenwich, Eng., Sep 7, 1533, 2:30PM LMT, per NN. (Most other bios. state birth occurred between 3-4PM.)

ELIZABETH II: London, Eng., Apr 21, 1926, 2:40AM BST, per London Times.

EMERSON, RALPH WALDO: Boston MA, May 25, 1803, 1:15PM LMT, from SS.

EUGENIE: Granada, Spain, May 5, 1826, 11:55AM, from SS.

FAIRBANKS, DOUGLAS: Denver CO, May 23, 1883, 9AM, per FN.

FALWELL, JERRY: Lynchburg VA, Aug 11, 1933, noon EST, per twin brother.

FERMI, ENRICO: Rome, Italy, Sep 29, 1901, 7PM MET, from Gau.

FISCHER, BOBBY: Chicago IL, Mar 9, 1943, 2:39PM CST, per BC.

FITZGERALD, F. SCOTT: St. Paul MN, Sep 24, 1896, 3:30PM CST, from SS.

FLYNN, ERROL: Hobart, Tasmania, Jun 20, 1909, 9:25PM from SS. (Birthplace has been corrected.)

FONDA, JANE: New York NY, Dec 21, 1937, 9:14AM EST, per BC.

FORD, BETTY: Chicago IL, Apr 8, 1918, 3:45PM CWT, from BC.

FORD, HARRISON: Chicago IL, Jul 13, 1942, 11:41AM, from BC.

FORD, HENRY: Dearborn MI, Jul 30, 1863, 7AM LMT, (biog. Olson)

FORD, HENRY II: Detroit MI, Sep 4, 1917, 6PM EWT per BC.

FORD, GERALD: Omaha NB, Jul 14, 1913, 12:43AM CST, from Baby book.

FOSSE, BOB: Chicago IL, Jun 23, 1927, 10:29PM CDT, per BC.

FRANCO, FRANCISCO: LaCoruna, Spain, Dec 4, 1892, 12:30AM LMT, per BC.

FRANK, ANNE: Frankfurt, Ger., Jun 12, 1929, 7:30AM (bio, Schnabel).

FRANZ FERDINAND: Graz, Austria, Dec 18, 1863, 7:45AM LMT, from NN.

FRANZ JOSEPH: Vienna, Austria, Aug 18, 1830, 8:23AM LMT, from SS.

FREDERICK THE GREAT: Potsdam, Ger., Jan 24, 1712, noon LMT, per MNN.

FREMONT, JOHN: Savannah GA, Jan 21, 1813, 11PM LMT, from Bible.

FREUD, SIGMUND: Pribor, Czech., May 6, 1856, 6:30PM LMT, from father's diary.

FURSTENBURG, DIANE VON: Brussels, Bel., Dec 31, 1946, 3AM GMT, from herself.

GABLE, CLARK: Cadiz OH, Feb 1, 1901, 5:30AM EST. (biog. Garceau)

GABOR, ZSA ZSA: Budapest, Hun., Feb 6, 1915, 8:08PM MET. (Time from her autobiography, year corrected from private sources.)

GALILEO: Pisa, Italy, Feb 15, 1564, 3PM LMT. (biog. Barbera)

GANDHI, INDIRA: Allahabad, India, Nov 19, 1917, 11:11PM, from AFA.

GANDHI, M. K.: Porbandar, India, Oct 2, 1869, 7:33AM LMT, from SS.

GANDHI, RAJIV: Poona, India, Aug 20, 1944, 8:11AM, per Nehru journals.

GARBO, GRETA: Stockholm, Swe., Sep 18, 1905, 7:30PM MET, per BC.

GARDNER, AVA: Smithfield NC, Dec 24, 1922, 7:10PM EST, per BC.

GARFIELD, JAMES: Orange Twp OH, Nov 19, 1831, 3:25AM LMT, from DCD.

GARIBALDI, GIUSEPPE: Nice, Fr., Jul 4, 1807, 6AM LMT, from AB.

GARLAND, JUDY: Grand Rapids MN, Jun 10, 1922, 6AM CST, per BC.

GAUDI, ANTONIO: Reus, Spain, Jun 25, 1852, 9:30AM from BC.

GAUGUIN, PAUL: Paris, Fr., Jun 7, 1848, 10AM LMT, from Gau., date corrected.

GELDOF, BOB: Dublin, Ire., Oct 5, 1951, 2:20PM BST, from himself.

GENET, JEAN: Paris, Fr., Dec 19, 1910, 10AM GMT, per BC.

GEORGE V: London, Eng., Jun 3, 1865, 1:18AM, from NN.

GEORGE VI: Sandringham, Eng., Dec 14, 1895 3:05AM. from SS.

GERSHWIN, GEORGE: New York NY, Sep 26, 1898, 11:09AM EST, from SS.

GETTY, JOHN PAUL: Minneapolis MN, Dec 15, 1892, 8:30AM CST, (biog. Hewins)

GIBSON, MEL: Peekskill NY, Jan 3, 1956, 4:45PM, from local newspaper.

GLADSTONE, WILLIAM: Liverpool, Eng., Dec 29, 1809, 9AM LMT, from SS.

GLEASON, JACKIE: New York NY, Feb 26, 1916, 2:13AM EST, per BC.

GODFREY, ARTHUR: New York NY, Aug 31, 1903, 2:30AM EST, from himself.

GOEBBELS, JOSEPH: Rheydt, Ger., Oct 29, 1897, 10:30PM MET, Gau. for date, time corrected from BC.

GOERING, HERMANN: Rosenheim, Ger., Jan 12, 1893, 4AM MET, from Gau.

GOETHE, WOLFGANG VON: Frankfurt, Ger., Aug 28, 1749, noon per autobio.

GOLDBERG, WHOOPI: New York NY, Nov 13, 1955, 12:48PM, from BC.

GORDON, CHARLES: Woolwich, Eng., Jan 28, 1833, 9:53AM LMT, per Bible.

GOYA, FRANCISCO: Fuentetodos, Spain, Mar 30, 1746, 11:30AM LMT, from AB.

GRANT, CARY: Bristol, Eng., Jan 18, 1904, 1:07AM, from SS.

GRANT, U. S.: Pt. Pleasant OH, Apr 27, 1822, 6AM LMT, from father.

GRIFFIN, MERV: San Mateo CA, Jul 6, 1925, 4:45AM PST, per BC.

GUEVARA, CHE: Rosario, Arg., Jun 14, 1928, 9:30PM, per BC.

HAMMARKSJOLD, DAG: Jonkoping, Swe., Jul 29, 1905, 11:30AM MET, from MMD.

HARDING, WARREN G.: Corsica OH, Nov 2, 1865, 2:30PM LMT, from DCD.

HARLOW, JEAN: Kansas City, MO, Mar 3, 1911, 7:40PM CST, per BC.

HART, GARY: Ottawa KS, Nov 28, 1936, 2:25PM CST, per BC.

HAUPTMANN, BRUNO: Kamenz, Ger., Nov 26, 1899, 1PM MET, from SS.

HAYDN, FRANZ JOSEF: Rohrau, Austria, Mar 31, 1732, 4PM LMT. (biog. Geiringer)

HEARST, WM. RANDOLPH: San Francisco CA, Apr 29, 1863, 5:58AM LMT, from SS.

HEFNER, HUGH: Chicago IL, Apr 9, 1926, 4:20PM CDT, per BC.

HELMS, JESSE: Monroe NC, Oct 18, 1921, 11AM EST, per BC.

HELMSLEY, LEONA: Marbletown NY, Jul 4, 1920, 6AM, from *Palace Coup* by M. Moss.

HEMINGWAY, ERNEST: Oak Park IL, Jul 21, 1899, 8AM CST. (biog. Baker)

HENRY VIII: Greenwich, Eng., Jun 28, 1491, 8:45AM LMT, from archives.

HEPBURN, KATHARINE: Hartford CT, Nov 8, 1907, noon EST, from herself.

HERZL, THEODOR: Budapest, Hun., May 2, 1860, 1:30AM LMT, per BC.

HESS, RUDOLF: Alexandria, Egypt, Apr 26, 1894, 10AM LMT, per BC.

HESTON, CHARLTON: Evanston IL, Oct 4, 1923, 7:55AM, per BC.

HEYDRICH, REINHARD: Halle, Ger., Mar 7, 1904, 3PM MET, from Gau.

HIMMLER, HEINRICH: Munich, Ger., Oct 7, 1900, 3:30PM MET, from Gau.

HINDENBURG, PAUL VON: Poznan, Pol., Oct 2, 1847, 2:59PM LMT, from SS.

HIROHITO: Tokyo, Jap., Apr 29, 1901, 10:10PM JST, from SS.

HITCHCOCK, ALFRED: London, Eng., Aug 13, 1899, 8PM GMT, from himself.

HITLER, ADOLF: Branau, Austria, Apr 20, 1889, 6:30PM MET, per BC.

HOFFA, JAMES: Brazil IN, Feb 14, 1913, 6:52AM CST, per BC.

HOLDEN, WILLIAM: O'Fallon IL, Apr 17, 1918, 5PM per BC.

HOLLANDER, XAVIERA: Soerbaja, Java, Jun 15, 1943, sunrise from herself.

HOLMES, JOHN: Columbus OH, Aug 8, 1944, 10PM, from BC.

HOOVER, HERBERT: West Branch IA, Aug 10, 1874, 11:12PM LMT, from DCD.

HOOVER, J.EDGAR: Washington DC, Jan 1, 1895, 7AM EST, from SS.

HUBBARD, L. RON: Tilden NB, Mar 13, 1911, 2AM CST, from SS.

HUBERTY, JAMES: Canton OH, Oct 11, 1942, 12:11AM EWT, per BC.

HUDSON, ROCK: Winetka IL, Nov 17, 1925, 2:15AM CST, per BC.

HUGHES, HOWARD: Houston TX, Dec 24, 1905, 11PM CST, from him to his astrologer.

HUGO, VICTOR: Besancon, Fr., Feb 26, 1802, 10:30PM LMT, from Gau.

HUXLEY, ALDOUS: Godalming, Eng., Jul 26, 1894, 12:01AM GMT, from family sources which state "very early morning", chart rectified.)

IACOCCA, LEE: Allentown PA, Oct 15, 1924, 5PM EST, per BC.

ISHERWOOD, CHRISTOPHER: Disley, Eng., Aug 26, 1904, 11:45PM GMT. (from autobiography)

IVAN THE TERRIBLE: Moscow, Rus., Aug 25, 1530, 6PM LMT. (biog. Payne)

JENNER, BRUCE: Mt. Kisco NY, Oct 28, 1949, 6:16AM EST, per BC.

JOAN OF ARC: Domremy, Fr., Jan 6, 1412, sunset. (biog. Denis)

JOFFREY, ANVER: Seattle, Wash., Dec 24, 1928, 6:43PM, from BC.

JOHN XXIII: Sotto il Monte, Italy, Nov 25, 1881, 10:15AM LMT, per BC.

JOHN PAUL I: Canale d'Agordo, Italy, Oct 17, 1912, 11:30AM MET, per BC.

JOHN PAUL II: Waduwice, Pol., May 18, 1920, 1:15PM MET. (Discepolo)

JOHNSON, DON: Flat Creek MO, Dec 15, 1949, 10:30PM CST, per BC.

JOHNSON, LADY BIRD: Karnack TX, Dec 23, 1912, noon per BC.

JOHNSON, LYNDON: Stonewall TX, Aug 27, 1908, daybreak per mother.

JONES, Rev. JIM: Lynn IN, May 13, 1931, 10PM CST, per BC.

JOPLIN, JANIS: Pt.Arthur TX, Jan 19, 1943, 9:45AM CWT, per BC.

JORDAN, MICHAEL: Brooklyn NY, Feb 17, 1963, 10:20AM EST, from him

JORGENSEN, CHRISTINE: New York NY, May 31, 1926, 1:40PM EDT. (From her autobiography, chart rectified.)

JUAN CARLOS: Rome, Italy, Jan 5, 1938, 1:15PM MET, per BC.

JUNG, CARL: Kesswill, Switz., Jul 26, 1875, 7:20PM LMT, from SS.

KEACH, STACY: Savannah GA, Jun 2, 1941, 7:15PM EST, per BC.

KELLER, HELEN: Tuscumbia AL, Jun 27, 1880, 4PM LMT, from SS.

KELLY, GRACE: Philadelphia PA, Nov 12, 1929, 4:58AM EST. (from Jess Stearn, BC reportedly has time of 5:31AM.)

KENNEDY, ETHEL: Chicago IL, Apr 11, 1928, 3:30AM, per BC.

KENNEDY, JOHN F.: Brookline MA, May 29, 1917, 3:15PM EST, from DCD.

KENNEDY, ROBERT F.: Brookline MA, Nov 20, 1925, 3:10PM EST, from Dell.

KENNEDY, TED: Boston MA, Feb 22, 1932, 3:58AM EST, from hospital.

KEROUAC, JACK: Lowell MA, Mar 12, 1922, 5PM EST. (biog. Charters)

KHRUSHCHEV, NIKITA: Kalinovka, Rus., Apr 17, 1894, 12:30PM. (Per the German newspaper, Die Neue Zeitalter.)

KING, MARTIN LUTHER JR.: Atlanta GA, Jan 15, 1929, 11:20AM CST, chart rectified from mother's statement "close to Noon."

KIPLING, RUDYARD: Bombay, India, Dec 30, 1865, 4:53PM LMT, from SS.

KISSINGER, HENRY: Furth, Ger., May 27, 1923, 5:30AM MET, per BC.

KOHL, HELMUT: Oggersheim, Ger., Apr 3, 1930, 6:30AM MET, per BC.

KRISHNAMURTI, JEDDU: Madanapalle, India, May 12, 1895, 12:25AM LMT, from SS.

LAFAYETTE, MARQUIS DE: Chavaniac, Fr., Sep 6, 1757, 3AM LMT, from family records.

LANDON, MICHAEL: Jamaica NY, Oct 31, 1936, 12:12PM EST, from BC.

LAWRENCE, D.H.: Eastwood, Eng., Sep 11, 1885, 9:45PM, per mother.

LEARY, TIMOTHY: Springfield MA, Oct 22, 1920, 10:45AM EST, from himself.

LEE, BRUCE: San Francisco CA, Nov 27, 1940, 7:12AM PST, per BC.

LEIGH, VIVIEN: Darjeeling, India, Nov 5, 1913, 5PM. (biog. Edwards)

LENIN, NIKOLAI: Ulyanovsk, Russia, Apr 22, 1870, 9:42PM LMT, from SS (Date corrected).

LENNON, JOHN: Liverpool, Eng., Oct 9, 1940, 6:30PM BST, per mother.

LESSEPS, FERDINAND DE: Versailles, Fr., Nov 19, 1805, 3:30PM LMT, time from BC, date corrected.

LIBERACE: West Allis WI, May 16, 1919, 11:15PM CWT, per BC.

LIDDY, G. GORDON: Brooklyn NY, Nov 30, 1931, 6AM EST, per mother.

LINCOLN, ABRAHAM: Hodgenville KY, Feb 12, 1809, 7AM LMT, from DCD

LINDBERGH, CHARLES: Detroit MI, Feb 4, 1902, 2:30AM CST, from SS.

LLOYD GEORGE, DAVID: Manchester, Eng., Jan 17, 1863, 8:55AM LMT, from BJA.

LONDON, JACK: San Francisco CA, Jan 12, 1876, 2PM LMT, from SS.

LONGWORTH, ALICE ROOSEVELT: Oyster Bay NY, Feb 12, 1884, 8:30PM EST, per biog. by Felsenthal.

LOREN, SOPHIA: Rome, Italy, Sep 20, 1934, 2:10PM, from BC.

LOUIS XIV: St.Germain, Fr., Sep 5, 1638, 11:22AM LMT. (biog.Cromie)

LOUIS XVI: Versailles, Fr., Aug 23, 1754, 5:55AM LMT, from NN.

LUTHER, MARTIN: Eisleben, Ger., Nov 10, 1483, 11PM LMT, per mother.

MAC ARTHUR, DOUGLAS: Little Rock AR, Jan 26, 1880, 10:13AM LMT, from SS.

MC CARTHY, JOSEPH: Grand Chute WI, Nov 14, 1908, 3PM per BC.

MC ENROE, JOHN: Wiesbaden, Ger., Feb 16, 1959, 10:20PM MET, per mother.

MC KINLEY, WILLIAM: Niles OH, Jan 29, 1843, 10:32PM LMT, per mother.

MAC LAINE, SHIRLEY: Richmond VA, Apr 24, 1934, 3:57PM EST, per BC.

MC PHERSON, AIMEE: Ingersoll Ont., Oct 9, 1890, 5:30PM EST, from SS.

MACHIAVELLI, NICCOLO: Florence, Italy, May 3, 1469, 11:30PM, per Fagan.

MADISON, JAMES: Pt. Conway VA, Mar 16, 1751, 11:30PM LMT, per Bible.

MADONNA: Bay City MI, Aug 16, 1958, 7:05AM EST, from Dell.

MANDELA, NELSON: Umtata, S. Afr., Jul 18, 1918, 3PM EET, per LMR.

MANSON, CHARLES: Cincinnati OH, Nov 12, 1934, 4:40PM EST, per BC.

MAO TSE TUNG: Shaoshan, China, Dec 26, 1893, 8AM LMT, from MMD.

MARCOS, FERDINAND: Sarrat, PI, Sep 11, 1917, 12:51AM, from Lanot.

MARCOS, IMELDA: Tacloban, PI, Jul 2, 1929, 2:30PM, from Lanot.

MARIA THERESA: Vienna, Austria, May 13, 1717, 7AM LMT, from archives.

MARIE ANTOINETTE: Vienna, Austria, Nov 2, 1755, 8PM LMT, from archives

MARIE OF ROMANIA: Eastwell, Eng., Oct 29, 1875, 10:28AM LMT, from SS.

MARTIN, BILLY: Berkeley CA, May 16, 1928, 3:43PM PST, per BC.

MARX, GROUCHO: New York NY, Oct 2, 1890, 8:35AM EST, per brother.

MARX, KARL: Trier, Ger., May 5, 1818, 2AM LMT, from FN.

MARY I: Greenwich, Eng., Feb 18, 1516, 4AM LMT, from archives.

MATA HARI: Leeuwarden, Neth., Aug 7, 1875, 2PM LMT, from BC.

MAX, PETER: Berlin, Ger., Oct 19, 1937, 2:30AM MET, from himself.

MAXIMILIAN: Vienna, Austria, Jul 6, 1832, 4AM LMT, from SS.

MEAD, MARGARET: Philadelphia PA, Dec 16, 1901, 9AM EST, from herself.

MEDICI, CATHERINE DE: Florence, Italy, Apr 13, 1519, 4:30AM LMT, from NN.

MENGELE, JOSEF: Gunzburg, Ger., Mar 16, 1911, 11:45AM MET, from BC.

MICHELANGELO: Caprese, Italy, Mar 6, 1475, 1:30AM LMT, from father

MIDLER, BETTE: Honolulu, HI, Dec 1, 1945, 2:19PM HST, per BC.

MIES VAN DER ROHE, LUDWIG: Aachen, Ger., Mar 27, 1886, 10AM per BC.

MILK, HARVEY: Queens Cty NY, May 22, 1930, 1:30AM EDT, from AA.

MITTERAND, FRANCOIS: Jarnac, Fr., Oct 26, 1916, 4AM per BC.

MONROE, MARILYN: Los Angeles CA, Jun 1, 1926, 9:30AM, per BC.

MONTANA, JOE: New Eagle PA, Jun 11, 1956, 3:25PM EST, per BC.

MONTGOMERY, BERNARD: London, Eng., Nov 17, 1887, 9:17PM GMT, per mother.

MOORE, MARCIA: Cambridge MA, May 22, 1928, 9AM EDT from herself.

MORE, SIR THOMAS: London, Eng., Feb 7, 1478, 3AM, per father's diary.

MORGAN, J.P.: Hartford CT, Apr 17, 1837, 3AM LMT, from SS.

MOUNTBATTEN, LORD: Windsor, Eng., Jun 25, 1900, 6AM GMT, from London Times.

MOZART, WOLFGANG AMADEUS: Salzburg, Austria, Jan 27, 1756, 8PM LMT, from FN.

MUHAMMAD ALI: Louisville KY, Jan 17, 1942, 6:30PM CST, per BC.

MURDOCH, RUPERT: Melbourne, Australia, Mar 11, 1931, 11:55PM, from himself.

MURPHY, AUDIE: Kingston TX, Jun 20, 1924, 7PM CST, per BC.

MURROW, EDWARD R.: Greensboro NC, Apr 25, 1908, 2AM EST, from MMD.

MUSSOLINI, BENITO: Dovia, Italy, Jul 29, 1883, 2PM LMT, per Gau.

NAPOLEON I: Ajaccio, Corsica, Aug 15, 1769, 10:35AM (Chart rectified, NN has 9:52AM, AB has 11AM, British Museum has 11:30AM.)

NAPOLEON III: Paris, Fr., Apr 20, 1808, 1AM LMT, from SS.

NEHRU, JAWHARLAL: Allahabad, India, Nov 14, 1889, 10:05PM LMT, from AFA.

NELSON, HORATIO: Norfolk, Eng., Sep 29, 1758, 10AM LMT, from MNN.

NERO: Rome, Italy, Dec 15, 37AD, 7AM LMT, from Suetonius.

NEWMAN, PAUL: Cleveland OH, Jan 26, 1925, 6:30AM EST, per BC.

NICHOLAS II: Tsarskoe Selo, Rus., May 18, 1868, 12:02PM, from SS.

NIGHTINGALE, FLORENCE: Florence, Italy, May 12, 1820, 2PM LMT, per BC.

NIXON, PAT: Ely NV, Mar 16, 1912, 3:25AM, from Boston Globe.

NIXON, RICHARD: Yorba Linda CA, Jan 9, 1913, 9:30PM PST, from nurse.

NORIEGA, MANUEL: Panama, Pan., Feb 11, 1935, 5AM EST, from Heliogram.

NORTH, OLIVER: San Antonio TX, Oct 7, 1943, 12:43AM CWT, per the Congressional Record.

NOSTRADAMUS: St.Remy, Fr., Dec 14, 1503, noon LMT, from NN.

NOVAK, KIM: Chicago IL, Feb 13, 1933, 6:13AM CST, per BC.

NUREYEV, RUDOLF: Irkutsk, Rus., Mar 17, 1938, 1PM. from D. Parker.

OMARR, SYDNEY: Philadelphia PA, Aug 5, 1926, 11:27AM EST, per BC.

ONASSIS, ARISTOTLE: Izmir, Tur., Jan 20, 1906, 10AM. per Church.

ONASSIS, CHRISTINA: New York NY, Dec 11, 1950, 3PM. per BC.

ONASSIS, JACQUELINE: Southampton NY, Jul 28, 1929, 2:30PM EDT, from library.

ONO, YOKO: Tokyo, Jap., Feb 18, 1933, 8:30PM JST, from Dell.

OSWALD, LEE HARVEY: New Orleans LA., Oct 18, 1939, 9:55PM per mother.

PADEREWSKI, IGNACE JAN: Kurylowka, Pol., Nov 18, 1860, 4AM LMT, per Mandala Zycia.

PAHLAVI, SHAH REZA: Teheran, Iran, Oct 26, 1919, 8:15AM ST, from MMD.

PASTEUR, LOUIS: Dole, Fr., Dec 27, 1822, 2AM LMT, from Gau.

PATTON, GEORGE: San Marino CA, Nov 11, 1885, 6:38PM PST. (biog.Farago)

PAUL VI: Concescio, Italy, Sep 26, 1897, 10:30PM MET, from AFA.

PENN, WILLIAM: London, Eng., Oct 24, 1644, 7AM LMT, from AFA.

PERON, EVITA: Los Toldos, Arg., May 7, 1919, 5AM. (biog. Montgomery)

PERON, JUAN: Lobos, Arg., Oct 8, 1895, 6:30AM per BC.

PEROT, H. ROSS: Texarkana TX, Jun 27, 1930, 5:34AM CST, per BC.

PETER THE GREAT: Moscow, Rus., Jun 9, 1672, 12:30AM LMT, from royal archives, biography by Massie states 1AM.

PHILIP, PRINCE: Corfu, Greece, Jun 10, 1921, 10AM EET. (biog. Judd)

PIAF, EDITH: Paris, Fr., Dec 19, 1915, 5AM GMT, from Gau.

PICASSO, PABLO: Malaga, Spain, Oct 25, 1881, 11:15PM GMT. (biog.Cabanne)

PICKFORD, MARY: Toronto, Ont., Apr 9, 1893, 3AM EST,.time from SS. (Year corrected)

PIKE, BISHOP JAMES: Oklahoma City OK, Feb 14, 1913, 3:30PM CST, per his wife.

PIUS XII: Rome, Italy, Mar 2, 1876, noon LMT, from SS.

POLANSKI, ROMAN: Paris, Fr., Aug 18, 1933, 2:47PM GMT, from CL.

POLK, JAMES KNOX: Mecklenburg NC, Nov 2, 17959, noon LMT, from DCD.

POMPADOUR, MME DE: Paris, Fr., Dec 29, 1721, 10AM per family records.

PRESLEY, ELVIS: Tupelo MS, Jan 8, 1935, 4:35AM CST, per BC.

PRICE, LEONTYNE: Laurel, MS, Feb 10, 1927, 6:15AM CST, per BC.

PRINCIP, GAVRILO: Gornji Obljaj, Yugo., Jul 13, 1894, 4:40PM per *Sarajevski Atentat* by Bogicevic.

PROUST, MARCEL: Paris, Fr., Jul 10, 1871, 11:30PM LMT, from Gau.

QUAYLE, DAN: Indianapolis IN, Feb 4, 1947, noon CST, per newspaper.

RAJNEESH, BHAGWAN: Gadawara, India, Dec 11, 1931, 5:13PM ST, from Dell.

RATHER, DAN: Wharton TX, Oct 31, 1931, 6:13PM CST, per BC.

RAY, JAMES EARL: Alton IL, Mar 10, 1928, 3PM CST, per BC.

REAGAN, NANCY: New York NY, Jul 6, 1921, 1:18PM, from her in a TV interview, mother says 1:30AM.

REAGAN, RONALD: Tampico IL, Feb 6, 1911, 2PM CST, from SS.

REDFORD, ROBERT: Santa Monica CA, Aug 18, 1936, 8:02PM PST, per BC.

REHNQUIST, WILLIAM: Milwaukee WI, Oct 1, 1924, 11:32AM CST, per BC.

RHODES, CECIL: Bishops Stortford, Eng., Jul 5, 1853, 7PM LMT, from SS.
RICHARD I: Oxford, Eng., Sep 8, 1157, 3AM LMT, from old manuscript.
RIGHTER, CARROLL: Salem NJ, Feb 2, 1900, 9AM EST, from himself.
ROBERTS, ORAL: Ada OK, Jan 24, 1918, 11:30AM CST, from autobiog.
ROBESPIERRE,MAXIMILIEN DE: Arras, Fr., May 6, 1758, 2AM LMT, from NN.
ROCKEFELLER, JOHN D.: Richford NY, Jul 8, 1839, 11:55PM LMT. (biog.Nevins)
ROCKEFELLER, NELSON: Bar Harbor ME, Jul 8, 1908, 12:10PM EST, from himself.
ROCKNE, KNUTE: Voss, Norway, Mar 4, 1888, 2PM per BC.
RODIN, AUGUSTE: Paris, Fr., Nov 12, 1840, noon LMT, from AB.
ROMMEL, ERWIN: Heidenheim, Ger., Nov 15, 1891, noon, from Gau.
ROOSEVELT, ELEANOR: New York NY, Oct 11, 1884, 11AM EST, per Bible.
ROOSEVELT, FRANKLIN D.: Hyde Park NY, Jan 30, 1882, 8:45PM LMT, per father's diary.
ROOSEVELT, THEODORE: New York NY, Oct 27, 1858, 7:45PM LMT. (biog. Lorant)
ROSS, DIANA: Detroit MI, Mar 26, 1944, 11:46PM EWT, per BC.
RUBINSTEIN, ARTUR,Lodz, Pol., Jan 28, 1887, 7:30AM LMT, per BC.
RUSSELL, BERTRAND: Trelleck, Wales, May 18, 1872, 5:45PM LMT. (biog. Wood)
RUSSELL, LILLIAN: Clinton IA, Dec 4, 1861, 10:50PM LMT, from SS.
RUTH, BABE: Baltimore MD, Feb 6, 1895, 1:45PM EST, per BC.
SADAT, ANWAR: Mit abu el Kom, Egypt, Dec 25, 1918, 12:15AM EET, Egyptian Embassy said between midnight and 12:30AM.
SAND, GEORGE: Paris, Fr., Jul 1, 1804, 10:25PM LMT, from SS.
SANDBURG, CARL: Galesburg IL, Jan 6, 1878, 12:05AM, per mother.
SCHUBERT, FRANZ: Vienna, Austria, Jan 31, 1797, 1:30PM, per father.
SCHUMANN, ROBERT: Zwickau, Ger., Jun 8, 1810, 9:30PM LMT, from SS.
SCHWARZKOPF, NORMAN: Trenton NJ, Aug 22, 1934, 4:45AM EDT, per BC.
SCHWEITZER, ALBERT: Kayserburg, Fr., Jan 14, 1875, 11:50PM, per BC.
SELLECK, TOM: Detroit MI, Jan 29, 1945, 8:22AM EWT, per BC.
SERLING, ROD: Syracuse NY, Dec 25, 1924, 3:15PM EST, from himself.
SERRA, JUNIPERO: Petra, Mallorca, Nov 24, 1713, 1AM LMT. (biog.Cullen)
SHELLEY, PERCY B.: Field Place, Eng., Aug 4, 1792, 10PM LMT, from family records.
SIEGEL, BUGSY: New York NY, Feb 28, 1906, 11:22PM EST, from MMD.
SINATRA, FRANK: Hoboken, NJ, Dec 12, 1915, 3AM EST, per mother.
SLICK, GRACE: Chicago IL, Oct 31, 1939, 7:37AM, per BC.
SMITH, JOSEPH: Sharon VT, Dec 23, 1805, 6PM LMT, time from NN chart rectified 15 min. earlier.
SPEER, ALBERT: Mannheim, Ger., Mar 19, 1905, noon LMT, per autobiog.
SPENCER, DIANA: Sandringham, Eng., Jul 1, 1961, 7:45PM BST, per mother.
SPIELBERG, STEVEN: Cincinnati OH, Dec 18, 1946, 6:16PM EST, per BC.
SPITZ, MARK: Modesto CA, Feb 10, 1950, 5:45PM PST, per BC.
STALIN, JOSEPH: Gori, Rus., Dec 21, 1879, 8:15AM LMT, per BC.
STEIN, GERTRUDE: Pittsburgh PA, Feb 3, 1874, 8AM LMT. (biog.Brinnin)
STEINBECK, JOHN: Salinas CA, Feb 27, 1902, 3PM PST. (biog.Valjean)
STEINEM, GLORIA: Toledo OH, Mar 25, 1934, 10PM EST, per BC.
STEVENSON, ADLAI: Los Angeles CA, Feb 5, 1900, 11:55AM PST, per the family maid.
STEVENSON, ROBERT LOUIS: Edinburgh, Scot., Nov 13, 1850, 1:30PM LMT, per baby book.
STOKOWSKI, LEOPOLD: London, Eng., Apr 18, 1882, 4AM GMT, from SS, year corrected.
STRAUSS, JOHANN: Vienna, Austria, Oct 25, 1825, 2AM LMT, per BC.
STREEP, MERYL: Summit NJ, Jun 22, 1949, 8:05AM, per BC.

STREISAND, BARBRA: Brooklyn NY, Apr 24, 1942, 5:08AM EWT, per BC.

SUTTER, JOHN: Kandern, Ger., Feb 15, 1803, 5AM LMT, from SS.

SWANSON, GLORIA: Chicago IL, Mar 27, 1899, 12:45AM, per SS.

SWAYZE, PATRICK: Houston TX, Aug 18, 1952, 8:10AM CST, from himself.

TAFT, WM. HOWARD: Cincinnati OH, Sep 15, 1857, 9:46AM, from SS.

TAYLOR, ELIZABETH: London, Eng., Feb 27, 1932, 8PM GMT, from herself.

TCHAIKOWSKY, PETER ILICH: Molotov, Rus., May 7, 1840, 6:35AM LMT, from SS.

TEMPLE, SHIRLEY: Sta.Monica CA, Apr 23, 1928, 9PM PST, per BC.

TERESA, MOTHER: Skopje, Yugo., Aug 27, 1910, 2:25PM MET, from the Astrologische Auskunftsbogen.

THATCHER, MARGARET: Grantham, Eng., Oct 13, 1925, 9AM GMT, from AFA.

THOMAS, LOWELL: Woodington OH, Apr 6, 1892, 7:30PM CST, from SS.

THOREAU, HENRY DAVID: Concord MA, Jul 12, 1817, 2PM LMT, from one of his poems.

TIBERIUS: Rome, Italy, Nov 16, 42BC, 11AM LMT, from old Latin manuscript.

TOKYO ROSE: Los Angeles CA, Jul 4, 1916, 6:08AM PST, from CL.

TOSCANINI, ARTURO: Parma, Italy, Mar 25, 1867, 2AM LMT, from SS.

TOULOUSE LAUTREC, HENRI DE: Albi, Fr., Nov 24, 1864, 6AM, from Gau.

TROTSKY, LEON: Yanovka, Rus., Nov 7, 1879, 10:09PM LMT, from SS.

TRUDEAU, PIERRE: Montreal, Que., Oct 18, 1919, 7AM EDT, from mother.

TRUMAN, HARRY: Lamar MO, May 8, 1884, 4PM CST, from DCD.

TURNER, TED: Cincinnati OH, Nov 19, 1938, 8:50AM EST, per BC.

TURNER, TINA: Brownsville TN, Nov 26, 1939, 10:10PM CST, from herself.

TWAIN, MARK: Florida MO, Nov 30, 1835, 4:45AM LMT, from SS.

URICH, ROBERT: Toronto OH, Dec 19, 1946, 9:40PM EST, per BC.

USTON, KEN: New York NY, Jan 12, 1935, 3AM EST, per his mother.

VALENTI, JACK: Houston TX, Sep 5, 1921, 8:30PM CST, per BC.

VALENTINO, RUDOLPH: Castallaneta, Italy, May 6, 1895, 3PM MET. per BC.

VANDERBILT, GLORIA: New York NY, Feb 20, 1924, 9:55AM. per autobio.

VAN GOGH, VINCENT: Zundert, Neth., Mar 30, 1853, 11AM LMT, per Gau.

VERDI, GIUSEPPE: Roncole, Italy, Oct 10, 1813, 8PM LMT, from SS.

VICTORIA: London, Eng., May 24, 1819, 4:15AM LMT, from SS.

VOLTAIRE: Paris, Fr., Nov 21, 1694, 5:30PM LMT, from AB.

WAGNER, RICHARD: Leipzig, Ger., May 22, 1813, 4AM LMT, from SS.

WALESA, LECH: Popovo, Pol., Sep 29, 1943, 3:30AM MET. per autobiog.

WALTERS, BARBARA: Boston MA, Sep 25, 1929, 6:50AM,.date from biog. by Oppenheimer, time from Lois Rodden.

WAMBAUGH, JOSEPH: Wilkinsburg PA, Jan 22, 1937, 6:50AM per BC.

WARHOL, ANDY: Pittsburgh PA, Aug 8, 1928, 6:30AM EST. (biog. Ultra Violet)

WARREN, EARL: Los Angeles CA, Mar 19, 1891, 2AM PST, from SS.

WASHINGTON, GEORGE: Wakefield VA, Feb 22, 1732, 10AM LMT, per Bible.

WELLES, ORSON: Kenosha WI, May 6, 1915, 7AM CST, per BC.

WELLINGTON, DUKE OF: Dublin, Ire., May 1, 1769, 11:55PM LMT, from MNN.

WHITE, DAN: Bellflower CA, Sep 2, 1946, 8:13AM PST, per BC.

WHITE, STANFORD: New York NY, Nov 9, 1853, 4:20PM LMT, from SS.

WHITE, VANNA: Conway, SC, Feb 18, 1957, 2:35PM EST, from autobiog.

WIESENTHAL, SIMON: Becazca, Pol., Dec 31, 1908, 11:30PM MET, per autobiography.

WILDE, OSCAR: Dublin, Ireland, Oct 16, 1854, 3AM LMT, per bapt. cert.

WILHELM II: Berlin, Ger., Jan 27, 1859, 2:45PM LMT, from archives.

WILLIAM OF ORANGE: The Hague, Neth., Nov 14, 1650, 9PM LMT, from NN.

WILSON, EDITH: Wytheville VA, Oct 15, 1872, 9AM, per autobiography.

WILSON, WOODROW: Staunton VA, Dec 28, 1856, 11:45PM LMT, from DCD.

WINDSOR, DUCHESS OF: Blue Ridge Summit PA, Jun 19, 1895, 10:30PM EST, time from doctor, year from biog. by Higham.

WINDSOR, DUKE OF: Richmond, Eng., Jun 23, 1894, 9:55PM GMT, per London Times.

WRIGHT, FRANK LLOYD: Richland Center WI, Jun 8, 1867, 8PM LMT, per documents at Columbia Univ.

YELTSIN, BORIS: Talitza, Russia, Feb 1, 1931, 11:50AM, per Lois Rodden's Data News 8/91.

YOGANANDA,Gorakhpur: India, Jan 5, 1893, 8:38PM LMT, from himself

YOUNG, BRIGHAM: Whitingham VT, Jun 1, 1801, 11AM LMT, from NN.

ABBREVIATIONS

AA	American Astrology magazine
AB	Andre Barbault, French astrologer
AFA	American Federation of Astrologers
BC	Birth certificate
BR	Birth record
Bible	Family Bible
BJA	British Journal of Astrology
CL	Church of Light in Los Angeles
DCD	Doris Chase Doane, book on US Presidents
Dell	Dell's Horoscope magazine
Ebertin	Institute of Cosmobiology in Germany
Fagan	Cyril Fagan, noted astrologer
FN	Famous Nativities by Maurice Wemyss
Gau	Michel Gauquelin, birth certificate data
Kraum	Ralph Kraum, American astrologer
MMD	Marion Meyer Drew, American astrologer
MNN	More Notable Nativities, pub. by Aries Press
NN	Notable Nativities by Alan Leo
LMR	Lois M. Rodden, birth certificate data
SS	Sabian Symbols by Marc Edmund Jones

LAS VEGAS, NV

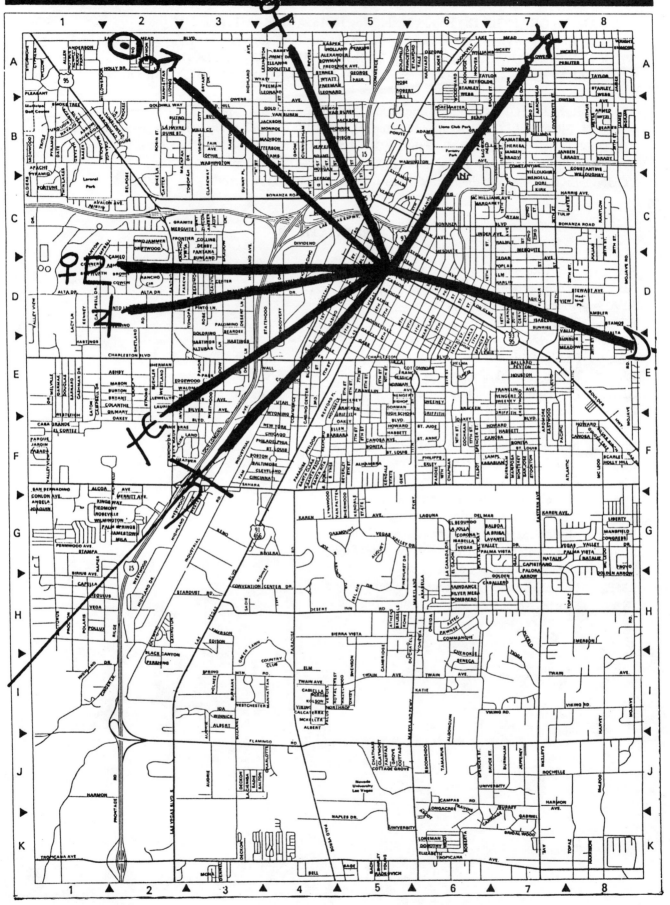

This first edition of
Bon Voyage: An Astrological Study of Relocation
was typeset and designed using WordPerfect,
a registered trademark of WordPerfect Corporation.
Body typeface is Marin 10 supplied by Publisher's Powerpak,
a registered trademark of Atech Software.